WRITER-FILES

General Editor: Simon Trussler

Associate Editor: Malcolm Page

File on
SHAFFER

Compiled by Virginia Cooke
and Malcolm Page

Methuen. London and New York

A Methuen Paperback
First published in 1987 as a paperback original
by Methuen London Ltd,
11 New Fetter Lane, London EC4P 4EE
and Methuen Inc, 29 West 35th Street,
New York, NY 10001

Copyright in the compilation
© 1987 by Malcolm Page and Virginia Cooke
Copyright in the series format
© 1987 by Methuen London Ltd
Copyright in the editorial presentation
© 1987 by Simon Trussler

Typeset in IBM 9pt Press Roman
By ⋏ Tek Art Ltd, Croydon, Surrey
Printed in Great Britain by
Richard Clay (The Chaucer Press) Ltd,
Bungay, Suffolk.

Contents

The theatre is, by its nature, an ephemeral art: yet it is a daunting task to track down the newspaper reviews, or contemporary statements from the writer or his director, which are often all that remain to help us recreate some sense of what a particular production was like. This series is therefore intended to make readily available a selection of the comments that the critics made about the plays of leading modern dramatists at the time of their production – and to trace, too, the course of each writer's own views about his work and his world.

In addition to combining a uniquely convenient source of such elusive *documentation*, the 'Writer-Files' series also assembles the *information* necessary for readers to pursue further their interest in a particular writer or work. Variations in quantity between one writer's output and another, differences in temperament which make some readier than others to talk about their work, and the variety of critical response, all mean that the presentation and balance of material shifts between one volume and another: but we have tried to arrive at a format for the series which will nevertheless enable users of one volume readily to find their way around any other.

Section 1, 'A Brief Chronology', provides a quick conspective overview of each playwright's life and career. *Section 2* deals with the plays themselves, arranged chronologically in the order of their composition: information on first performances, major revivals, and publication is followed by a brief synopsis (for quick reference set in slightly larger, italic type), then by a representative selection of the critical response, and of the dramatist's own comments on the play and its theme.

Section 3 offers concise guidance to each writer's work in non-dramatic forms, while *Section 4*, 'The Writer on His Work', brings together comments from the playwright himself on more general matters of construction, opinion, and artistic development. Finally, *Section 5* provides a bibliographical guide to other primary and secondary sources of further reading, among which full details will be found of works cited elsewhere under short titles, and of collected editions of the plays – but not of individual titles, particulars of which will be found with the other factual data in Section 2.

The 'Writer-Files' hope by striking this kind of balance between information and a wide range of opinion to

5

offer 'companions' to the study of major playwrights in the modern repertoire — not in that dangerous pre-digested fashion which can too readily quench the desire to read the plays themselves, nor so prescriptively as to allow any single line of approach to predominate, but rather to encourage readers to form their own judgements of the plays in a wide-ranging context.

Peter Shaffer had a box-office success with his first stage play, *Five Finger Exercise*, in 1958 at the age of 32 — significantly, with just a few more years of life-experience behind him than such near-contemporaries as Osborne, Arden, or Wesker, all of whom had their theatrical breakthroughs at a younger age. Shaffer wrote, seemingly, in a more traditional form — that of the well-made drawing-room play — and on the no less traditional but seemingly outmoded subject of the small agonies of middle-class domesticity. Now, in the late-1980s, he is best recognized as a writer of epic-scale dramas at a time when the West End is once again full of plays about . . . the small agonies of middle-class domesticity.

Shaffer is thus, paradoxically, both a successful commercial dramatist, yet one who makes technical demands in his plays which require the taking of 'uncommercial' risks — such as only a subsidized national company is nowadays prepared to take. No less paradoxical, arguably, is his use of 'epic' not to explore the social truths that Brecht required of the form, but to put into a sweepingly ambitious perspective the psychological exploration of individual sensibilities. Some of the critics represented in this volume have suggested that his use of dazzling spectacle can blind audiences to essentially commonplace attitudes towards the human predicament: and certainly, in *Shrivings*, when Shaffer reverted to a narrowly domestic setting for a 'universal' debate, the result was for many a severe disappointment. Yet he remains one of our very few dramatists able to command with assurance *all* the resources of the stage, with an almost Elizabethan feeling for the impact — and the relevance — of the visual dimension of theatre.

As the range of views represented in this volume reminds us, he arouses fiercely conflicting passions from the critics — and as his own writings assembled here demonstrate, he is highly articulate about his own intentions and the craftsmanship with which he gives them shape. He expresses, interestingly, a liking for the term *playwright*, whose very spelling stresses that the dramatist is a *maker* rather than just a writer of plays; and it is in this sense that Shaffer himself has made a distinctive contribution to the contemporary theatre.   Simon Trussler

1926   15 May, born in Liverpool, twin brother of Anthony, also a playwright. 'My father was a property company director, a North countryman. My mother came from Devonport. We were [in Liverpool] till I was nine. I went to prep. school there and then we all moved to London in 1936. We were in London for a couple of years. Then the war came and from that point we were peripatetic. I went to the Hall School in Hampstead and then to St. Paul's.' (Interview with Brian Connell, 1980.)

1944-47   Conscripted as a 'Bevin Boy'. 'For two and a half years I was down Chislet colliery in Kent. I can't say it was pleasant. I worked some of it underground, but my eyes are very bad and I finally ended up on the surface doing haulage. That involved emptying ten ton trucks of carbide and rock, very good for the muscles, not very good particularly for anything else. . . . My three years in coalmining gave me an enormous sympathy and feeling of outrage in contemplating how a lot of people had to spend their lives.' (Interview with Brian Connell, 1980.)

1947-50   Exhibition to Trinity College, Cambridge. BA in History. Co-edited *Granta*, student magazine, with his brother.

1951   Publication of *The Woman in the Wardrobe*, first of three detective novels written pseudonymously and jointly with his brother.

1951-54   Lived and worked in New York. 'I sold books in Doubleday's shop. I worked in the airlines terminal. I worked in Grand Central Station, in a department store, Lord and Taylors, and then I moved to the New York Public Library in the acquisitions department. That meant that I ordered books for the library, a slightly boring job, in fact a very boring job. . . . I soon discovered after a year or so that the librarian's life was not for me. It's much too orderly and dreary. . . . I had absorbed the belief that if I really wanted to do something, the theatre for example — I was passionately devoted to the theatre — that was somehow frivolous and wrong and bad for me. I should do something respectable and "serious" like one of the professions and the theatre in my spare time. As a result I think I denied myself the pleasure of writing plays for a very long time.' (Interview with Brian Connell, 1980.)

1954-56 Back in London, worked for Boosey and Hawkes, music publishers. 'I didn't see my future in terms of a factory making brass band instruments in Edgware or indeed anywhere else. So I resigned and said, well, I'll live now on my literary wits.' (Interview with Brian Connell, 1980.) *The Salt Land,* television play, 1955. Literary critic for weekly review *Truth,* 1956-57.

1957 *The Prodigal Father* on radio, and *Balance of Terror* on television.

1958 *Five Finger Exercise,* first stage play, a big success.

1961-62 Music critic for *Time and Tide.*

1962 Double bill, *The Private Ear* and *The Public Eye,* staged in London.

1964 *The Royal Hunt of the Sun* at Chichester Festival prior to opening at National Theatre, London.

1965 *Black Comedy* at Chichester Festival and National Theatre, London. Divides his time between living in Manhattan and in England. 'New York excited me. I found it a marvellous contrast to England. I like the balance of the extraordinary urban electricity of New York and the profound experience of the English countryside.' (Interview with Brian Connell, 1980.)

1967 *White Lies* opens in New York, with *Black Comedy.*

1968 *White Liars* (a revision of *White Lies*) in London.

1970 *The Battle of Shrivings* in London.

1973 *Equus* at National Theatre, London.

1979 *Amadeus* at National Theatre, London.

1985 *Yonadab* at National Theatre, London.

Five Finger Exercise

Play in two acts.

First London production: Comedy Th., 16 July 1958
(dir. John Gielgud; with Roland Culver as
Mr. Harrington, Adrianne Allen as Louise, Brian
Bedford as Clive, Michael Bryant as Walter, and Juliet
Mills as Pamela; re-directed by Peter Wood, 1959).

First New York production: Music Box, 2 Dec. 1959
(dir. John Gielgud; London cast, except for Jessica
Tandy as Louise).

Film version: adapted (to Carmel, California) by Frances
Goodrich and Albert Hackett, 1962 (dir. Daniel
Mann; with Jack Hawkins as Mr. Harrington, Rosalind
Russell as Louise, and Maximilian Schell as Walter).

Published: London: Hamish Hamilton, 1958; New York:
Harcourt Brace, 1959 (with preface by Frederick
Brisson); and in *Plays and Players*, Sept. 1958,
p. 25-30, and Oct. 1958, p. 26-31. *Revised version* (as
played in New York): in *New English Dramatists, 4*
(Penguin, 1962); in *Three Plays: Shaffer, Wesker,
Kops* (Penguin, 1968); in *Three Plays* (Penguin, 1976);
and in *Collected Plays* (1982). The changes in the
revision are minor.

*Walter, a young German student, arrives in the Suffolk
weekend cottage of the upper-middle-class Harringtons,
to act as tutor to the fourteen-year-old daughter, Pamela.
He has good relations at first not only with his pupil,
but also with Clive, the confused, drinking undergraduate
brother, and the intellectually under-nourished wife,
Louise Harrington. Clive has previously been the focus
of hostility between Louise and her husband, a furniture
manufacturer, proudly philistine and contemptuous of
his wife's artistic interests. Walter, very sensitive and
repudiating his own family for its Nazi past, becomes the
scapegoat for the whole family. Accused of trying to
make love to Louise, he unsuccessfully attempts suicide.*

Five Finger Exercise might seem a bit evasive now, but Clive himself was genuinely confused about what he wanted. I don't believe all that much has changed with the change in sexual attitudes. The agony of discovering the truths of life for yourself remains much as ever.

Shaffer, quoted in Oleg Kerensky, *The New British Drama* (London, 1977), p. 56

I have very little recollection how I wrote *Five Finger Exercise;* the experience of writing disappears once you have lived through it. It's a semi-autobiographical play, and it's what's called 'well-made'. I don't think a play can be 'well-made' enough; but you should conceal your own cleverness, your own 'making' of the play. I like plays to be like fugues — all the themes should come together at the end.

Shaffer, quoted in Kerensky, as above, p. 58

In London, where it was first done, audiences were confronted with what was then the conventional West End drawing-room set — chintz on the sofa; offstage piano; drinks on the sideboard — only here used to contain not a light comedy but a scene of considerable domestic violence. Family war raged in that safe-seeming drawing-room; and the contrast was considered to be shocking. When I did it [in New York], although the play was much liked it was found acceptable for other reasons; in fact, almost the opposite ones from those prevailing in London. In New York a play which was found somewhat outrageous by English audiences was always being praised here for its restraint; for its good manners!

Shaffer, *Dramatists Guild Quarterly,* Spring 1980, p. 29

It is (I almost blush to record it in these days) a family play, and that family is (now indeed I do blush) both English and middle class. What distinguishes it is the treatment. Mr. Shaffer can write, and can write well enough to bring new life to familiar situations. The English middle-class family is certainly a long fought-over emotional battlefield. But the skirmishes are new to each set of participants, and what we require of a playwright is that he makes his new for us. Mr. Shaffer does. The conflict in his conventional family may be conventional. But then such conflicts are. The point is that he has the ability to give them depth. Not depth of complexity but depth in time. From the very first we feel that this group of people has been really living together, scraping against each other, year after year. We come in at a chosen point in a continuous history. The past vibrates in the present, and it is this which makes for the kind of reality that really matters in a play about a family. . . . Shaffer's dialogue has pace and bite though no great wit. His faults are glibness and whimsy. But he has kept his suburban cabbage patch to almost window-box size — and every leaf and caterpillar is minutely observed.

T.C. Worsley, *New Statesman,* 26 July 1958, reprinted in *Plays in Review, 1956-1980,* ed. Gareth and Barbara Lloyd Evans (London, 1985), p. 68-9

The playwright examines a frustrated household of ostensibly well-to-do and happy people. True, Mr. Harrington, who has made the money, is touchy about being thought common. Mrs. Harrington is compensating for a not very happy marriage by becoming an intellectual snob. The son, just up at Cambridge, is dangerously like 'a mother's boy', to put it no more plainly. The pony-loving adolescent daughter is probably the least tangled. And the catalyst? A smooth, mature young German tutor, who gives himself out as an orphan. He worships this family of his adoption; and they batten on him — rather as some tongue-tied families will use a dog to test otherwise inadmissible feelings and attitudes of affection. Slowly, much too slowly, the ugliness of the pattern of jealousies and loneliness is opened up — to be brought to a violent and by no means ineffective breaking point. What then is missing? The ability to create sympathy. Mr. Shaffer can analyze his rather pathetically shallow characters persuasively enough. But between 'pathetic' and 'sympathetic' there is that all important inch — which is never crossed here, unless it is so momentarily by the son of the house (Brian Bedford) and the enigmatic German romantic. . . . It did not catch me up into emotional surrender or belief.

Philip Hope-Wallace, *Manchester Guardian,* 17 July 1958; reprinted in *Plays in Review, 1956-1980,* p. 70

It turns out to be an unusually skilful and unexpected foray of new ideas and new perceptions into the fustiest stronghold of convention; having convinced the old-fashioned West End play-goer that it is 'all right' — not sordidly concerned with the kitchen sink, and certainly not in any way experimental, but just an ordinary play about people like you and me – it proceeds bit by bit to strip its characters and their way of life bare with as much ruthlessness as Ionesco sets about rather the same business in *The Bald Prima Donna.* Only here the weapon is psychological penetration: Shaffer takes the typical Dodie Smith-Esther McCracken family . . . and instead of accepting them as the self-evident, indisputable *données* upon which a light comedy or drama can be based, he asks us to look at them, consider why they are as they are, and what would happen if suddenly something unexpected, from outside their normal experience, should intrude on the settled picture of complacent mediocrity. . . .

Taken line by line there is nothing at all surprising or upsetting about Shaffer's style: it is just the usual pruned, heightened realism of traditional stage parlance. But if we look at the play as a whole it at once becomes apparent that the action does not progress, as one would expect, by way of conversations leading purposefully towards clear stages in the dramatic argument; instead, the play organizes itself into a series of splendid self-revealing tirades, usually directed at the passive, uninvolved head of Walter, who remains so mysterious (necessarily to his function in the play) precisely because he alone of the characters is not permitted to reveal himself in this way. . . .

John Russell Taylor, *Anger and After*
(London, revised ed., 1969), p. 274-5

His characters belong to the most vulnerable of all sections of our society, targets of contempt from above, envy from below, and sharp shooting from their own intelligent young . . . a group which invites derision. But it does not get it from Shaffer. . . . *Five Finger Exercise* is firmly placed in a strong tradition of English plays, leading down from Pinero and Granville Barker by way of Noel Coward and *The Vortex;* a tradition in which the clash of generations is not a background to heroic personal disaster but the play's major preoccupation.

J.W. Lambert, 'Introduction', *New English Dramatists, 4*
(Penguin, 1962), p. 9-10

The play is not drawing-room but Attic, and intimates as much by its allusions to the Greek tragedies which Clive Harrington, the son of the family, peruses at Cambridge. Oedipus remains discreetly unmentioned, but vulgar Mrs. Harrington half-recalls seeing a play where the hero put out his own eyes just before she withdraws with her son to the sofa for mutual caresses. Like Phaedra, both she and Clive carry lying tales to Mr. Harrington in a bid to pay out Walter, the young German tutor, for resisting their advances. Accordingly Walter succeeds to the tragic destiny of Hippolytus. While its tight design confirms a debt to Greece, the play is still Christian, though strictly a celebration for Easter. . . . A new version of the Passion story, reminiscent of *The Idiot*, it illustrates the murderous loathing mankind feels when brought face to face with goodness. Walter undergoes a resurrection, another link with the gods of the Easter rituals, on being dragged from his gas-filled room by the repentant Harringtons. No doubt they would soon wish they had left him where he was.

John Carey (on the BBC TV production), 'Oh Come All Ye Separate,' *The Listener*, 31 Dec. 1970, p. 928

The Private Ear

Play in one act.

First London Production (with *The Public Eye*): Globe Th., 10 May 1962 (dir. Peter Wood; with Douglas Livingstone as Ted, Terry Scully as Bob, and Maggie Smith as Doreen).

First New York production (revised version): Morosco Th., 9 Oct. 1963 (dir. Peter Wood; with Barry Foster as Ted, Brian Bedford as Bob, and Geraldine McEwan as Doreen).

Film version retitled *The Pad (and How to Use It)*: adapted to Venice, California, in screenplay by Thomas Ryan and Ben Webb, 1966 (dir. Brian G. Hutton; with Brian Bedford as Bob, James Farentino as Ted, and Julie Sommers as Doreen).

Published (with *The Public Eye*): London: Hamish Hamilton, 1962; New York: Stein and Day, 1964; London and New York: Samuel French, 1964; in *Four Plays* (Penguin, 1981); and in *Collected Plays*.

Set in a shabby bed-sitting room in London, The Private Ear *refers to the ear of Bob, an awkward, sensitive, and lonely young man with a passion for classical music. Having met a girl at a concert and assumed that she shares his love for music, he has invited her home to dinner – his first date. His worldly-wise friend and co-worker at the import-export office, Ted, has agreed to cook the dinner and serve as social coach for the inexperienced Bob. But when Doreen arrives, she turns out to be ignorant about*

13

music (she was given the concert ticket and didn't want to waste it), full of clichés, and more compatible with the flashy and superficial Ted than with Bob, who is hopeless at small talk. The evening is predictably disastrous for Bob. When finally left alone with Doreen, he plays the Love Duet from Madame Butterfly, *which softens Doreen enough to allow a kiss, but she rejects his ardent, clumsy pass at her. As she leaves, Bob gives her Ted's address. Left alone, he deliberately scratches the record and stands listening to the damaged music of the Love Duet.*

The Private Ear was written in four days, probably why I've never been happy with it. It was written over for the American production. . . . [The critics] said I identified myself with Ted, who is a working-class snob. If anything, I identify myself with Bob, the other boy. Of course I wasn't happy about it. There was some cheap knock-about comedy in it. But the critics who didn't like the double bill, didn't take it for what it was intended. A *jeu d'esprit.* After all, this is a privilege of writers. Anouilh has his *pièces roses* and *pièces noires.* In many ways it was a breakthrough for me.

Shaffer, in *Behind the Scenes,* p. 206

Each of the plays [*The Private Ear* and *The Public Eye*] had three characters and was concerned with aspects of love. In the first of them, I was undeniably persisting in my hopes of being pitied in public; the misunderstood and maladroit Bob was close to my heart. . . . Playwrights, after all, have to match actors in being encyclopedias of human experience. They have to dig inside themselves and discover what in them also belongs to their neighbours. I suspect that my initial sense of being invisible in the world and of having been too careful with my youth paralleled similar feelings in many of my audiences. . . . The mime at the end of the first one was received with breathless amusement. . . . Both featured the young Maggie Smith and really established her as the finest comedienne of her generation.

Shaffer, 'Preface' to *Collected Plays,* p. ix

[*The Private Ear* and *The Public Eye*] are very funny, at moments deeply moving, always entertaining, and both essentially serious. It is all too rare to experience moments of sheer delight in the theatre, but at the end of *The Private Ear,* as Terry Scully and Maggie Smith, in beautifully timed and acutely observed performances, falter their way to making love while the Love Duet from Madame Butterfly fills the squalid attic room, one could have stood and cheered − if it had not been so intensely moving. . . . It is the idealist, the visionary, who in that one evening sees in himself the animal instincts he despises in his friend and this realization shatters his hopes and dreams.

Michael Wall, *The Guardian,* 11 May 1962

In England nothing is more difficult to write about than a class lower than your own . . . and Peter Shaffer falls straight into the trap in the first part of his double bill. . . . We are invited to scoff at their gastronomic gaucheness and their hopeless attempts to comprehend high bourgeois art and on the opening night the gallery, that hot-bed of proletarian conservatism, responded with predictable guffaws when the hero, casting about for works to attract his beloved, hits on something as fancifully esoteric as *Peter Grimes.* The tone throughout is sickeningly condescending, like that of certain Noel Coward sketches in the 'thirties. Mr. Shaffer takes pains to exhibit a mastery of lower-class idiom that he transparently hasn't got.

Kenneth Tynan, *The Observer,* 13 May 1962

The twin comedies that go by the combined title of *The Private Ear* and *The Public Eye* are delightful any way you want to look at them, and I want to look at them as the work of a gambling man. Author Peter Shaffer doesn't care what kind of chances he takes.

In the first, and possibly the happier of the two . . . he throws three entirely different moods into the dice box and defies you to say, as you watch them tumble, that they don't add up to a coherent number. For convenience, let's give these moods names: the Skirmish, the Scramble, the Scratch.

The Skirmish is what takes place while Brian Bedford, whose face manages to look as uncombed as his hair does, does his level best − with the help of a most unhelpful friend − to entertain a girl in his attic flat. The flat is not very spiritual, but he is sure that the girl is. . . . Now that it is absolutely clear that Mr. Bedford is a fellow of imagination and taste, light years ahead of the cretins who have come together across his dinner table, something else happens. He is left alone with the girl for a moment and in a

15

last desperate gesture he puts Puccini on the stereo amplifiers that fill his tilted attic roof. The rest is silence, and hilarious. . . . Though this Scramble has all logic against it . . . it wins its own victory hands down. Peter Wood has staged it with the finesse of a mildly deranged ballet, and the lunges toward the cot, majestic in their clumsiness, are lovely. . . . If the little play is, in any plausible sense, a sequence of three emotional nonsequiturs, it works as a piece of clever music might, in movements that assert themselves as contrast.

Walter Kerr, *New York Herald Tribune,* 10 Oct. 1963

The sexual theme, amusingly handled in itself, gains interest by mirroring the sociological. In this lower-middle-class milieu the hero's atypical love of serious music and his hi-fi, the pandering friend's donjuanism, the girl's specious respectability, all become attempts, ludicrous or pathetic, to ascend socially. The funny sexual skirmish is part of the class war. It is all done with good humour, exemplary economy of means, and a sympathy that never strays into either sogginess or smart-aleckry.

John Simon, *The Hudson Review,* Winter 1963-64; reprinted in *Uneasy Stages* (Random House, 1975), p. 26

Shaffer's development as a playwright is demonstrated in his frank use at two points in the play of expressionistic devices. To cover the lapse in time − the duration of the dinner − the three diners 'freeze', and a condensed version of the dialogue is heard from a prerecorded tape. The conversation seems to be entirely between Ted and Doreen, speeded up at times to 'a high-pitched gabble'. This is apparently the way the evening sounds to Bob's private ear.

Warren Sylvester Smith, 'Peter Shaffer', *Dictionary of Literary Biography,* XIII (Detroit, 1982), p. 455

On the film

The Pad (and How to Use it) . . . is a squirming title for an excrutiating film, drawn and quartered from Peter Shaffer's one-act play, *The Private Ear.* This boy's musicality is phantom, and he conducts imaginary orchestras, which seem to have become Hollywood's tactful way of hinting at impotence. . . . The dialogue appears to be conducted in front of a hidden script-conference of boneheads. . . .

Penelope Gilliatt, *The Observer,* 23 Sept. 1966

Ross Hunter, the Hollywood production genius who gave the world *Tammy* and a yock-pile of fill'ems starring Rock Hudson and Doris Day, has actually produced an intelligent picture at last. . . . Bedford, the only hold-over from the Broadway cast, is the perfect mouse – funny when he squeaks, staggering when he roars. . . . Farentino with never a false step leads the spectator to the clear-eyed conclusion of this wise little comedy: people who use people are the loneliest people in the world.

Time, 2 Sept. 1966

The Public Eye

Play in one act.
First London production (with *The Private Ear*): Globe Th., 10 May 1962 (dir. Peter Wood; with Kenneth Williams as Julian, Richard Pearson as Charles, and Maggie Smith as Belinda).
First New York production: Morosco Th., 9 Oct. 1963 (dir. Peter Wood; with Barry Foster as Julian, Moray Watson as Charles, and Geraldine McEwan as Belinda).
Film version: released in Britain as *Follow Me,* in the USA as *The Public Eye,* screenplay by Peter Shaffer, 1971 (dir. Carol Reed; with Michael Jayston as Charles, Topol as Julian, and Mia Farrow as Belinda).
Published (with *The Private Ear*): London: Hamish Hamilton, 1962; London and New York: Samuel French, 1962; New York: Stein and Day, 1964; in *Four Plays* (Penguin, 1981); and in *Collected Plays.*

Charles Sidley, a successful but stuffy middle-aged accountant, has hired a detective to report on the fidelity of his young wife, Belinda, a former waitress whom he has unsuccessfully tried to make over into his own image. The private detective is Julian Christoforou, a zany Greek fellow with a sweet tooth, who eats sugared yoghurt and munches macaroons. The play takes place in Sidley's office, where Julian reports on his month's surveillance of Belinda. She has, according to the report, a penchant for grade-C horror films and a developing passion for a man to whom she has never spoken, but who keeps following her. He is, of course, the detective. In a surprising twist, Julian convinces Sidley that the only way to save his marriage is to change places with the detective – to trail Belinda for a month, neither of them speaking,

17

and let her show her husband how to enjoy life with spontaneity. In the meantime, Christoforou, weary of watching others' private lives but having none of his own, will quit the spy business and take over the accountant's office.

Christoforou was played by the coruscating Kenneth Williams, and I would stand at the back of the theatre night after night just to experience the hysterical accuracy with which he would explode every line of his closing scene – an object lesson in comic timing. Alas, the New York performance . . . was curtailed almost at the start by the asssassination of President Kennedy some seven weeks after the play opened. The prevailing mood of the city was scarcely conducive to comedy, and though the *New York Times* hailed *The Public Eye* as soaring like an unfettered bird, the grim mood of the time soon shot it down to earth, along with its romantic companion.

Shaffer, 'Preface' to Collected Plays, p. ix

The surprises which Mr. Shaffer draws continuously out of the second story . . . are supple enough to make a telescope look clumsy, and a set of Chinese boxes positively puerile. . . . It is in the character of this detective, who eats macaroons and knows by glittering intuition how to avoid a horror film or fool the Inland Revenue, that the histrionic challenge of the play lies. The husband and the wife are entirely credible; it is he who has to be unbelievable as well. In him the piece becomes a naturalistic fantasy, a solidly real dream, a day-to-day unicorn. . . . This man, this faun, is played by Kenneth Williams. . . . Whether he is in the margin of Pan or the routine of a travelling salesman, Mr. Williams's touch is certain, his control of the shifting mood of the play absolute.

Harold Hobson, Christian Science Monitor, 12 May 1962

The first scene is written too whimsically, and Kenneth Williams intensifies this impression by making the detective so conscious of his own amusing eccentricities (such as the tendency to picnic off macaroons in the middle of a conversation), but as the play gets more serious, both it and Kenneth Williams's performance improve until they end, hand in hand, quite magnificently. . . . The marriage broke up, for example, because the accountant had tried so hard to force his wife into his own sober image her reaction had been to go to endless horror films alone, which is why he sniffed a lover and hired a detective. . . . This idea is a brilliantly serious piece of fantasy and it is backed up by many more direct moral precepts, always put with the same lightness. One of them could stand as a motto for a critic: 'There is no sin more unpardonable than denying that you were pleased when pleasure touched you — you can die for that.'

> Bamber Gascoigne, 'Touched by Pleasure', *The Spectator,*
> 18 May 1962, p. 653

The Public Eye is a more ambitious affair, and though it has wonderful exuberance, and ample comic invention, it does ultimately miss the mark. It cannot quite decide whether it wants to be Peter Sellers's type of farcical comedy verging on dropping pants, or something more metaphysical and 'absurd' in the manner of Ionesco, which leads to contradictions and eventual wobbliness. I can willingly suspend my disbelief or believe in unwilling suspenders, but I cannot do both at once. Absurdist farce is as possible as farcical absurdity, but one or the other element must predominate and set the tone.

> John Simon, *Hudson Review,* Winter 1963-64; reprinted in
> *Uneasy Stages* (Random House, 1975), p. 26-7

Half of Peter Shaffer's new loaf, which was unwrapped last night at the Morosco Theatre, is tastier than six baked by less gifted men. *The Public Eye* . . . is a specimen of an art that has become so rare that it ought to be kept under glass. It is high comedy that is not only comic but also gay, sophisticated, and wise. It soars and sings with the enchantment of a happy, unfettered bird. Mr. Shaffer's moral — and all high comedy worth the name has a moral — is nothing new. He is preaching the enjoyment of life and love while one is lucky enough to have them. . . . A man of impeccable logic, Christoforou, if you don't begin to wonder whether he is a man at all. He describes himself at one point as the third party always looking in at other peoples' lives. But isn't he, as Mr. Shaffer has written him and as Barry Foster lightly and whimsically plays him, a fantastic guardian angel, a kind of earthy, laughing, adult amorino, temporarily in human guise?

> Howard Taubman, *New York Times,* 10 Oct. 1963

Mr. Foster's role [Christoforou] is like the last ace turned up in two-handed bridge. Halving a grapefruit with a flick of a wrist and

19

sending a fountain of yogurt ceilingward at the slightest opportunity, he is a symphony of scratches, peerings, parings, twitches, and extremely noisy salt-cellars. . . . The part, with all of its busy comic extravagance, is wrapped around a nice meaty kernel of comment, comment on the virtue of silence between companionable people and upon the fondness conspiracy can breed. The actor sobers himself to this additional task most adroitly and while he is on stage (which is for about half of the playlet) the contentment out front is enormous.

Walter Kerr, *New York Herald Tribune,* 10 Oct. 1963

On the film

It doesn't take . . . long for *The Public Eye* to go to pieces, amiable and attractive though it be. Adapted by Peter Shaffer from his own one-act play, the screenplay attempts to expand his original concept to feature-length dimensions simply by adding what is essentially travelogue footage. While I bow to no one in my affection for London, there is a tremendous difference between using its distinctive locales as, say, Alfred Hitchcock did in *Frenzy,* where parks, clubs, hotels, and the environs of Covent Garden added organically to his story, and turning the city into so much cotton batting to pad out a woefully thin little tale.

Arthur Knight, 'A Patrolman for All Seasons',
Saturday Review, 19 Aug. 1972, p. 69

It doesn't seem that such a relationship can endure, although we are made to endure every cloying moment of it in *The Public Eye.* He (Michael Jayston) is a highly paid English tax accountant; she (Mia Farrow), a slightly wilted California flower-child marooned in London en route home from Katmandu. . . . After the wedding she begins to realize that her Pygmalion is rather stuffy, and he sees that his Galatea is resisting the finer things he is trying to offer her. . . . The film would be a laughable travesty were it not directed by Carol Reed, who made such superb films as *The Third Man, Odd Man Out* and *Outcast of the Islands.* That makes it a sad travesty.

J.C., *Time,* 11 Sept. 1972

The Merry Roosters Panto

Christmas entertainment, with songs by Stanley Myers.
First London production: Wyndham's Th., 19 Dec. 1963 (dir.
Joan Littlewood, and performed at matinees by the cast of
Oh, What a Lovely War!, presented at the same theatre in the
evenings).
Revived: The Place, London, 26 Dec. 1969 (dir. Joan Littlewood).
Unpublished.

The framework is once more the pierrot concert party, but now bent on lighter things. Against the same old red-white-and-blue bulbs, they tell a modern-dress version of Cinderella, with an added villain called Redsocks, the Theatre Manager (in fact the company's manager, Gerry Raffles, in a welcome return to the footlights), a mustachio'd brute with top-hat and cigar who is out to stop the panto taking place on his premises. He hates panto and he hates children: the Roosters therefore invite the audience to keep cave, to hiss, boo, and shout warnings whenever the villain comes in sight, so that they can make themselves scarce. Redsocks contrives to trap the Roosters at the Ball – which is being held in honour of a Cosmonaut, Prince X – and takes them all back to school, where he tyrannizes them in a mortar-board. But Cinders frees them by disguising herself as a school inspector, and at last she gets her prince and a trip to the moon.

As pantos go, *The Merry Roosters* is undeniably jolly, and the kids – egged on by what sounded like carefully planted hecklers in their midst – soon took a keen and vocal delight in it. . . . Shaffer's best creations are the Duchess of Margate (a sub-standard fairy godmother blessed with the gusty amiability of Avis Bunnage) and the ugly sisters Eartha and Dumpy. . . . There are traditional gags ('Do you know any good henchmen?' – 'I know a place where men hench all night') and some nice left-wing ironies, as when Miss Bunnage assures us that 'Duchesses only help those who help themselves'. There are also, it's true, some very uninspired passages, but the slapstick is continually ripe, and the right cosy, noisy interplay is created between stage and audience. All one wonders is why the panto – with a company and theatre to hand, and months of time to prepare it – should have reached the public in such a messy and blatantly under-rehearsed state.

Roger Gellert, 'People's Panto', *New Statesman*,
27 Dec. 1963

The Royal Hunt of the Sun

Play in two acts.

First British production: by the National Th., at Chichester
Festival Th., 7 July 1964; transferred to the Old Vic Th.,
8 Dec. 1964 (dir. John Dexter; with Colin Blakely as Pizarro,
Robert Stephens as Atahuallpa, Robert Lang as Old Martin,
and Michael Turner as De Soto; with music by Marc
Wilkinson).

First New York production: ANTA Th., 26 Oct. 1965 (dir. John
Dexter; with Christopher Plummer as Pizarro, David Carridine
as Atahuallpa, George Ross as Old Martin, and John Vernon
as De Soto).

Revived: Prospect Co. at the Round House, London, Aug. 1973,
preceded and followed by national tour (dir. Toby Robertson
and Eleanor Fazan; with Trevor Martin as Pizarro and Rupert
Frazer as Atahuallpa).

Film version: screenplay by Philip Yordan, 1969 (dir. Irving
Lerner; with Robert Shaw as Pizarro and Christopher Plummer
as Atahuallpa).

Opera: by Iain Hamilton, performed by the English National
Opera, Coliseum, London, 30 Mar. 1977 (with Geoffrey Chard
as Pizarro and Tom McDonnell as Atahuallpa).

Published: London: Hamish Hamilton, 1964; in *Plays and
Players,* Sept. and Oct. 1964; New York: Stein and Day, 1965;
New York: Ballantine, 1966; London: Samuel French, 1968;
London: Longman, 1968, ed. John W. Macdonald and John
C. Saxton, with introduction by A.W. England; London: Pan,
1969; in *Collected Plays,* 1982; ed. Peter Cairns, with personal
essay by Shaffer, Longman, 1983. *Opera libretto* by Iain
Hamilton published: Bryn Mawr, Pa: Theodore Presser, 1982.

*The play is narrated by old Martin Ruiz, the former page of
Francisco Pizarro, who in 1529 made his expedition to Peru in
search of gold and fame. In Act One ('The Hunt'), Pizarro recruits
soldiers from rural Spain. He promises gold, while Valverde, the
chaplain, promises souls: they will Christianize the heathens.*

Although Pizarro warns young Martin that there's no glory in soldiering, the young idealist enlists and they set out for Peru and the kingdom of the Incas, ruled over by Atahuallpa, their king and the sun-god's representative on earth, who ignores the bad omens and the warnings of his advisors. Believing Pizarro to be the White God, he allows the Spanish troops to approach the holy city of Cajamarca. They endure the forest, then ascend the Andes (Scene Eight is entitled 'The Mime of the Great Ascent'), and await the appearance of the Incan man-god. Met in great ceremony by the unarmed Incas, the Spaniards mercilessly slaughter the Incas and take Atahuallpa prisoner – a scene mimed to the accompaniment of cries and drums. At the end of the act, 'dragged from the middle of the sun by howling Indians, a vast blood-stained cloth bellies out over the stage'. In Act Two ('The Kill'), Old Martin recounts the developing relationship between Pizarro, a 63-year-old atheist, and his 33-year-old captive, who even now retains the impeccable dignity of a king. Over the objections of De Soto, Pizarro promises Atahuallpa his freedom if the large sun-room of his temple is filled with a ransom of gold. For two months, the Incas bring rare treasures, which the Spaniards will melt down into portable gold bars. Meanwhile the priests try to convert Atahuallpa, who prefers his own god and 'father', the sun. While growing greed causes tension among the soldiers, Pizarro becomes increasingly engaged with his prisoner, in whom he hopes to find 'an answer for Time'. When the room is filled with gold, Pizarro, who cannot gain assurance that his soldiers will be spared, must break his word and kill Atahuallpa. The Inca assures Pizarro that he cannot be killed, that he will rise again with the rising sun, a myth which Pizarro wants desperately to believe. Atahuallpa is tried, convicted, and garotted by the soldiers. The play ends as the Indians, 'robed in black and terracotta, wearing the great golden funeral masks of ancient Peru', finally despair when their dead king fails to rise with the sun. Pizarro is left holding and weeping over Atahuallpa's body.

The play simply narrates the conquest from the landing of Pizarro to the death of the last Inca Atahuallpa. That is what it does. What it is about is quite another question. You see, I first came on the subject some years back when . . . I was absolutely rivetted by [Prescott's *Conquest of Peru*]. The whole drama of the confrontation of two totally different ways of life: the Catholic individualism of the invaders, and the complete communist society of the Incas. . . . A fascinating subject, and I can't imagine why no dramatist or film-maker seems to have been drawn to it before. Well, my play might have been about that, but it isn't, or only very slightly. When I first wrote it it was much more historical, much too historical. . . . But gradually it evolved, rather like one of those series of drawings by Picasso which start with a very literal, minute realistic rendering of the subject and then gradually strip and simplify it until you are left with only the bare essentials. . . .

Briefly, it is a play about two men: one of them is an atheist, and the other is a god. That isn't just a camp way of putting it; it is literally true. Pizarro is, like most orthodox religious people, in practice an atheist: he believes, vaguely, in God, but sees him as something right outside the universe and essentially irrelevant to it and to everyday dealings in the world. Atahuallpa, on the other hand, is a god: to his people he is ruler, master, and immediately the source of all benefits, and also the embodiment of the sun, the giver of all life. . . . The play is about the relationship, intense, involved and obscure, between these two men, one of whom is the other's prisoner: they are so different, and yet in many ways — they are both bastards, both usurpers, both unscrupulous men of action, both illiterate — they are mirror images of each other. And the theme which lies behind their relationship is the search for god — that is why it is called 'The Royal *Hunt* of the Sun' — the search for a definition of the idea of god. In fact the play is an attempt to define the concept of god: a nice, modest little theme for any play to tackle!

Shaffer, interviewed by John Russell Taylor,
Plays and Players, April 1964

Why did I write *The Royal Hunt*? To make colour? Yes. To make spectacle? Yes. To make magic? Yes — if the word isn't too debased to convey the kind of excitement I believed could still be created out of 'total' theatre. . . . I did deeply want to create, by means both austere and rich — means always disciplined by a central aesthetic — an experience that was *entirely and only theatrical.* . . . I saw the active iron of Spain against the passive feathers of Peru: the conflict of two immense and joyless powers. . . . The conquistadores deified personal will; the Incas shunned it. Both in a deep sense denied man. . . .

The neurotic allegiances of Europe, the Churches and flags, the armies and parties, are the villains of *The Royal Hunt. . . .* Pizarro, like all men, is entangled in his birth. He too is without joy. In his negation he is as anti-life as the bitter church and the rigid sun are in their affirmations. . . . To separate worship from codification is almost as hard as to separate sex from violence, but surely it must be done. . . . He is left with no answers, ultimately with no existence. But in no very paradoxical sense he recovers joy, by finding real grief. The frost melts. As Genet said 'To see the soul of a man is to be blinded by the sun.'

Shaffer, 'Introduction' to The Royal Hunt of the Sun
(New York, 1964)

Take the Inca play. I felt more and more inclined to draw the character Pizarro, who is a Catholic, as an atheist, or at least as a man who explores what and who he is. When the church is revealed to him as being wicked and suspect, and loyalty, friendship, is revealed as being suspect and wicked, he has a feeling of the meaninglessness of life. It is this: what can one ultimately find to give one strength and stability?

Shaffer, in Behind the Scenes, p. 207-8

The setting by Michael Annals was unforgettably distinguished. It consisted of a metal disc hung high above the bare boards, incised with swords to form a Christian cross. At the moment the action of the play moved to Peru, this disc slowly opened outward to cries of 'Inca!' and turned into a gigantic petalled sun containing in turn Atahuallpa's court, his prison, and his treasure house, and which was finally ripped apart by the looting Spaniards to hang spoiled and blackened as a dreadful symbol of his ruined empire. People who saw this extraordinary production still talk feelingly of their memories – of the stylized massacre at the end of Act One, when a vast cloth of scarlet vomited from the throat of the sun to lie over the stage like a sinister lake of blood; of the ritual feeding of the Inca to the sound of tiny bells; of the roping of the Inca; of his execution and awaited resurrection, with a stage full of golden funerary masks in the darkness of predawn turning anguished triangular eyes toward an audience which seemed to share their desperate expectation that he would rise again. . . . I do not think that I ever enjoyed doing anything so much as *The Royal Hunt of the Sun* . . . I knew then that it was my task in life to make elaborate pieces of theatre. . . .

Shaffer, 'Preface' to Collected Plays, p. x-xi

25

When we did *Royal Hunt of the Sun,* we used a lot of costumes — we drowned the stage with gold and feathers, and when we came to solve the end of the play . . . we found we had exhausted all those effects. And I was looking at those extraordinary gold funeral masks of the Incas, those ones with long triangular eyes, and we suggested to each other that it would be interesting to use them. I'll never forget the first time they arrived in the theatre . . . and the transformation that happened on stage. When there were sixteen of them at the end, when they were all assembled around the stage, the temperature in the house rose enormously. And later, when the audience came out of the theatre, they said — how did one get the masks to reflect joy, hope, gloom, and change expression? And what, of course, was happening was not that the masks changed in any way — what was happening was that the changes to the communal imagination and emotion of the audience were being invested in those masks.

Shaffer, interviewed by Peter Adam,
The Listener, 14 Oct. 1976

In London the character of Atahuallpa, god-king of Peru, was played by Robert Stephens, who had made a considerable name for himself as an actor in what might be called middle-class English parts. Suddenly here he was appearing at the National Theatre in the feathered cape and golden costume of an exotic, shrieking, androgynous savage, half-bird and half divinity. . . . For English audiences Stephens appeared to be dazzlingly foreign, daringly weird, and very remote. The success my play enjoyed was partly based on the originality and fascination of this performance. . . .

When the play came [to New York] of course, the nature of the part seemed far less odd to audiences. The average New Yorker is reasonably familiar with Indian chiefs of one kind or another, and that familiarity inevitably trimmed something of the unexpectedness which in England had been one of the most noteworthy features of the part. The sea-change here did not aid my Inca king at all. He appeared on stage, I think, before an audience prepared to make a quite different connection with him than the one made in England by the denizens of Chichester or the Waterloo Road! Cajamarca appeared a very far-off place to the English audience; to Americans, I suspect, it appeared to be not too far from Cheyenne.

Shaffer, in *Dramatists Guild Quarterly,* Spring 1980

This giant drama, seen earlier this year at Chichester, has now moved into the National Theatre's London home, and a third seeing confirms and strengthens my belief that no greater play has been written and produced in our language in my lifetime. That is a large statement and it is a large play that calls it forth. . . . Its theme is large, to begin with it tells the almost incredible (yet true) story of the conquest of the mighty Inca Empire of Peru by a tiny handful of Spaniards under Pizarro in the sixteenth century. The Incas had peace, stability, and gold. The Spaniards had courage, avarice and guns.

And Christ. . . . Mr. Shaffer's indictment of the conquistadores who beat men's brains out with the cross seems even more savage now, yet no more answerable. . . . Yet this is not a pessimistic play, which is another of the large things about it. It is a humanistic hymn, an agnostic affirmation. . . . And Mr. Shaffer's faith — that it is in man that such goodness, truth, and beauty as the world affords is to be found — is expressed in language that clothes his theme in majesty.

Bernard Levin, Daily Mail, 9 Dec. 1964

This is possibly too vast a subject to fit on to any stage. In his treatment of it Mr. Shaffer has thrown in, with almost insolent boldness, every technique available to him, every dodge ever known to have been dramatically effective in the history of drama. There are dancing and mime, and a narrator, and a chanting chorus and musique concrete and eerie jungle sounds proceeding from all over the theatre. . . .

The qualities in which the play is on the whole short are beauty of language and profundity, as opposed to importance, of argument. This is not to say that there are not some very effective passages between Pizarro and the Inca, Pizarro and the priests that accompanied his expedition, Pizarro and his young page, a believer still in the virtues of honour. . . .

This is one of the most beautiful productions I have seen for a long time. The brilliant, bizarre costumes of the Peruvian Indians . . . are stirred into glorious movement in Claude Chagrin's choreography. The first opening of the golden disc of the sun to reveal the radiant figure of the Inca; the massacre of the Inca's guards; the moment when Pizarro's men fight with gold ingots while the menacing noises of the jungle sound from above them — these are moments of great theatre.

B.A. Young, Financial Times, 8 July 1964; reprinted in
The Mirror up to Nature (Kimber, 1982), p. 22

Peter Shaffer's new play is mightily ambitious. As vast in intention as the Andes mountains, in which his Inca Indians wait for their Spaniards, and the Spaniards shiver at them and the snow. Not only does he deal with colonialism; not only with the Church and civilization; he deals with personal values, with time, with god, with resurrection. Even Shakespeare didn't attempt all this in one play, and Mr. Shaffer's shoulders are, frankly, too slim.

Theatrically, the National Theatre's production feels its three and a half hours' length; there are blotches of tedium, digressions, repetition, and a general feeling of muddle. More importantly, there seems to be some essential hollowness. . . . Why then does one emerge with a sense of having absorbed so much of lasting value? It seems to me that there is no particular originality in Mr. Shaffer's ideas, and no particular feeling for the characters except as projections of ideas. *The Royal Hunt of the Sun* is too consciously 'about things'. As theology or philosophy, it is not much more searching than a decent undergraduate discussion, and cleverly wielded dramatic images cannot make it otherwise.

Benedict Nightingale, *The Guardian*, 8 July 1964

There is a visionary glory to *The Royal Hunt of the Sun* which transcends all ordinary theatre. Even so, a blind man would be exhilarated by the magnificent drama. . . . He would love it for the symmetry of its poetry, the musical grandeur of its noble speech and the shining strength of its wisdom. . . . The wonder is that these visual and aural effects never overpower or submerge the drama, never reduce the play to a pageant. As Pizarro and the Inca, Atahuallpa, come to know each other, affection grows between these two defiant bastards. . . . It is father-son, or god-to-god, because Pizarro pretends for a while that he is divine. . . . Thus the play tends to focus more and more on a single concept – honour. The conquest of Peru becomes the defeat of decency, and the betrayal of trust is the anguished cry that pierces to the bones of this noble encounter. . . . No Englishman in this century, save Shaw and Christopher Fry, has achieved such sensible beauty, such noble clarity of ideas. *The Royal Hunt of the Sun* might well be a masterpiece.

Norman Nadel, *New York World Telegram*, 27 Oct. 1965

It is not until the Spanish predator has begun to become spiritually linked to his proud but too confident victim that Mr. Shaffer's pageant acquires a face, a direct voice, a troubling sense of person.

Before that, and for a long first act of preparatory fencing about with shadows, we have had to be content with the sheen of bronze, the shrill cries of unseen birds, the separate meditations of unseen voices. . . .

In time a spiritual relationship — which is for Pizarro a spiritual despair — unites the two men as well. Pizarro, despising his mortality as he does, cannot believe in immortality. But he is fascinated by the Inca's faith that, even if he is garroted, he will swiftly be reborn: the sun always does that to its children. And so Mr. Plummer's Pizarro will stand, at the end, over a masked black-robed band of keening faithful as they solemnly beat out the sounds that promise to resurrect their king. He stares at the folly of another man's faith, and sees in it the death of his own fleetingly resurrected last hope.

It is in these scenes that Mr. Plummer is virtually perfect — wily, ratchety, defiant, wistful. And Mr. Carradine, once he has got past the vocal strain of all the earlier declamatory passages, is a haughty, naive, inquisitive, and attractively perplexed foil.

Certain of author Shaffer's points are handsomely abrasively visualized as the forlorn contest moves forward. To watch the gold of the Inca empire being torn loose from its majestic moorings — a giant sunburst of daggers is dismantled before our eyes — is to be faintly sickened. The language of the play has less impact than this boldly literal image.

Walter Kerr, *New York Herald Tribune,* 27 Oct. 1965

Colin Blakely's rugged Pizarro is not in search of organized human bliss. He is not even, though in the first instance he thinks he is, in search of gold. The gold he found. . . . But the gold corroded in his pockets, as the sublime Atahuallpa showed him, by the mere assertion of divinity, what he really desired. The force that drove on Pizarro with a contemptible handful of followers into a presumably hostile land with millions of soldiers in it was the hope that he would come again to believe, as he had believed in his poverty-stricken youth in Spain, that a man could die and on the third day rise again.

Harold Hobson, *The Sunday Times,* 13 Dec. 1964

But in the end, Shaffer is no more a theologian than he is a historian. The tragedy is a personal one. There are few scenes in modern drama as moving as that of the broken Spanish commander trying to sing a song that Atahuallpa had taught him: 'It's over, lad, I'm coming after you. . . . We'll be put into the same earth, father and son in our own land.'

Warren Sylvester Smith, 'Peter Shaffer',
Dictionary of Literary Biography, XIII, p. 458

About fifteen minutes into its second half, *The Royal Hunt of the Sun* ceases to be an expensive piece of costume jewellery and belatedly becomes a short but interesting drama. . . . The first half, in which Pizarro and his Spaniards stumble through jungle and ice-field to the Inca Shangri-La, never had any dramatic function. . . . All the charge and tension in their relationship come from the Inca and to recognize the part's demands is to marvel more than ever at the magnificence with which Stephens meets them.

He begins as a singing mask, chanting in abstract, melodious cries imperious as a peacock's, but with a wild, plaintive fall to his cadences. The mask is taken from him at his capture, and beneath it is revealed a man half-bird, crested and strutting like a golden pheasant, furious in captivity but too untamed for fear. . . . He dances for Pizarro like a mating bird of paradise, beaked and hieratic as a hunter in an Assyrian frieze. Stephens never loses the strangeness, the inhumanity, of the sun-god who truthfully says that he needs no one — even at his most pitiful, he keeps part of the royal hostage beyond sympathy — but at the same time slowly, wonderfully, unfurls the ideal manhood which tempts Pizarro to believe it can defeat even death. In the use of both voice and body, in its imaginative range and intelligence, the performance is . . . unique, self-generating and memorable. If *The Royal Hunt* survives as more than a feathered-and-gilt Christmas souvenir for this generation of schoolchildren, it will be for its one great role and its performer.

Ronald Bryden, 'Firebird', *New Statesman,*
18 Dec. 1964, p. 972

On the film

Shaffer's eventual involvement in film-making arose as a defensive response, not out of zeal. A specific turning point was reached because of the unbelievably bad film made of *The Royal Hunt of the Sun*. That fiasco proved a painful but effective learning experience for Shaffer. During interview sessions in 1980, I asked Shaffer what involvement he had with that movie. His response was blunt: 'Nothing. It taught me a lesson, in a way. I mean, I

shall never not do my own films again. It was terrible.'
C.J. Gianakaris, 'Drama into Film: the Shaffer Situation',
Modern Drama, XXVIII (March 1985), p. 87

General Francisco Pizarro (Robert Shaw) was, the way screen-writer Philip Yordan tells it, obsessed by his own bastardy. . . . In the bizarre personage of King Atahuallpa (Christopher Plummer) Pizarro encounters a man of his own kind, an implacable and almost superhuman force. . . . The eventual and inevitable execution of Atahuallpa becomes a pat symbol of Pizarro's psychosis, at once too easy and too unwieldy to be taken seriously.

Still, the proceedings . . . are well managed by director Irving Lerner in a style that might be called Eisenstein modern, and devotees of the Hollywood spectacular will cherish the bravado of the two leading actors. Robert Shaw bellows and glowers in his ornate armour like a psyched-up Errol Flynn. Christopher Plummer, in cloak, loincloth, gold necklaces, and flowing hair, looks like the lead singer of a particularly exotic rock group, and his attempts at a Peruvian dialect occasionally make him sound like one. His performance is unabashed camp, consisting about equally of ego, bluff, and plain old spam.

Time, 17 Oct. 1969

I didn't like Peter Shaffer's play at the National, but I had hopes of the film. . . . The Spanish Court, the agonizing voyage to Peru, the Inca temples, the terrifying and mysterious Peruvian land-scape, all would surely be great stuff for the cinema. The director, Irving Lerner, and screenwriter, Philip Yordan, obviously thought otherwise. Apart from a few shots of presumably Peruvian moun-tains, the picture could have been — surely must have been — entirely shot in the Seville and Madrid studios. A picture which might have been packed with splendid visual antics has become Verbal Cinema at its most loquacious.

Penelope Mortimer, *The Observer,* 4 Oct. 1969

A selection of other articles and reviews
Jules Glenn, 'Twins in Disguise: a Psychoanalytic Essay on *Sleuth* and *The Royal Hunt of the Sun', Psychoanalytic Quarterly,* XLIII (1974), p. 288-302.
Nick Lapole, 'Pizarro Invades Broadway', *New York Journal-*

American, 24 Oct. 1965, p. 23L [on technical staging difficulties].

Barbara Lounsberry, 'God-Hunting: the Chaos of Worship in Peter Shaffer's *Equus* and *The Royal Hunt of the Sun'*, *Modern Drama,* XXI (1978), p. 13-28.

P.L. Podol, 'Contradictions and Dualities in Artaud and Artaudian Theater: the "Conquest of Mexico" and the Conquest of Peru', *Modern Drama,* XXVI (1983), p. 518-27.

Simon Trussler, 'Peter Shaffer: *The Royal Hunt of the Sun'*, *Notes on Literature,* No. 142 (British Council, 1973).

K.H. Westarp, 'Myth in Peter Shaffer's *Royal Hunt of the Sun* and in Arthur Kopit's *Indians'*, *English Studies,* LXV (1984), p. 120-8.

Black Comedy

Farce in one act.

First London production: by the National Th. at Chichester Festival Th., 27 July 1965 (a double bill with Strindberg's *Miss Julie*); transferred to the Old Vic Th., 8 Mar. 1966 (dir. John Dexter; with Derek Jacobi as Brindsley, Louise Purnell as Carol, Maggie Smith as Clea, and Albert Finney as Harold).

Revived (with *White Liars*): Lyric Th., 21 Feb. 1968 (dir. Peter Wood; with James Bolam as Brindsley, Angela Scoular as Carol, Liz Fraser as Clea, and Ian McKellen as Harold); and (with final version of *White Liars*), Shaw Th., 28 June 1976 (dir. Paul Giovanni; with Peter Machin as Brindsley, Gemma Craven as Carol, and Celia Bannerman as Clea).

First New York production (with *White Liars*): Ethel Barrymore Th., 12 Feb. 1967 (dir. John Dexter; with Michael Crawford as Brindsley, Lynn Redgrave as Carol, Geraldine Page as Clea, and Donald Madden as Harold).

Published: in *Plays and Players,* April 1966; New York: Stein and Day, 1967 (as *Black Comedy, including White Lies);* with *White Liars,* London: Samuel French, 1967; London: Hamish Hamilton, 1968; revised and re-written, New York: Samuel French, 1968; in *Four Plays* (Penguin, 1981); and in *Collected Plays.*

The action takes place in the apartment of Brindsley Miller, a struggling young sculptor. He and his dithery fiancee Carol nervously await the arrival of two guests – Carol's stuffy military father, and George Bamberger, a millionaire and art collector who is to look at Brindsley's work. To impress both visitors, they have borrowed some antique furniture from Brindsley's vacationing neighbour and friend Harold, with the intention of replacing it before he returns. When a fuse blows, plunging the apartment building into darkness, the evening's complications begin – as does the overriding theatrical joke in Black Comedy, the reversal of light and darkness: thus, the play begins in total darkness, but when the fuse blows, the stage is flooded with light. The characters grope about in this 'darkness', in full view of the audience, and whenever a match is lit, the stage lights dim. Besides Carol's father, the other characters who arrive uninvited are Miss Furnival, a prudish spinster from upstairs who sips gin in mistake for lemonade, Brindsley's former girlfriend, Clea, who is bent on reclaiming her lover, and the neighbour, Harold, unexpectedly returned early from his trip. Brindsley must therefore make certain that all lights remain extinguished while he deftly returns the borrowed furniture from right under the noses (and bottoms) of his guests before Harold finds out. One further confusion is the mistaking of the electrical repairman for the rich art collector. When the electrical power is restored at the end of the play, the stage is once again blacked out. Shaffer sums up the evening in this stage direction: 'For the place, as for its owner, the evening is a progress through disintegration.'

Black Comedy is almost all gesture. You could almost put plate glass between the audience and the stage and still something comic would emerge from the acted play. I love high comedy and I love farce and I would love to do more of it. . . . It was the Chinese who thought of the idea behind *Black Comedy*. I went once to the Palace Theatre in London and saw the Peking Opera. They did an excerpt from a play called *Where Three Roads Meet.* . . . It is supposed to be pitch darkness, except it is all done in brilliant light, light so ferocious that it almost suggests darkness. The warrior gropes for his sword and challenges the intruder. They fight with swords so sharp they seemed . . . to cut little bits off the fringes of their clothing. Real swords. The effect on the audience was extraordinary, because it was wildly funny and wildly dangerous as well, so that they were caught between two emotions of alarm and delight.

Shaffer, interviewed by Brian Connell, 1980

In composing *Black Comedy,* I encountered one serious problem. The reversal of light and dark was not in itself a sufficiently sustaining idea to keep the play going for the required length. In actuality, someone would, of course, produce a candle and end the situation. What was needed was a reason for one of the people to *keep* the others in the dark. From this necessity arose the actual plot: the idea that the host had borrowed all the furniture in the room from an antique-collecting neighbour without telling him and that on the unexpected appearance of this dangerous neighbour the poor host had to return every scrap of it — chairs, tables, lamps, even a sofa — in the dark and unaided, before he could restore the light which would otherwise expose him as a thief. The gods really blessed me with this solution. The resultant sequence of furniture moving created some seven minutes of continuous laughter. Indeed the first night turned into a veritable detonation of human glee. A stern-looking middle-aged man sitting directly in front of me suddenly fell out of his seat into the aisle during this section of the play and began calling out to the actors in a voice weak from laughing, 'Oh stop it! Please, stop it!' I cannot remember a more pleasing thing ever happening to me inside a theatre.

Shaffer, 'Preface' to *Collected Plays,* p. xii-xiii

Peter Shaffer's *Black Comedy,* at the Chichester Festival Theatre, turns out to be an uproarious piece of slapstick vaudeville which makes play with the famous 'Duel in the Dark Room' which is one of the oldest turns of the Chinese theatre and which we saw when the Peking Opera was over here. . . . To watch an engaged couple, an ex-mistress, the girl's suspicious father, and a handful of unwanted neighbours or expected celebrities fumbling about in the dark mistaking one for another and generally arriving at some painful home truths is sometimes a little long but it comes to a magnificent climax almost worthy of Feydeau. Among the happiest studies in this farcical romp are a tipsy spinster by Doris Hare, a vengeful aesthete by Albert Finney, and Miss Maggie Smith as the ex-mistress impersonating a charwoman in the dark and spilling the beans to the future bride.

Philip Hope-Wallace, *The Guardian,* 28 July 1965

Peter Shaffer's *White Liars* and *Black Comedy* are two plays on the same theme but with a staggeringly different impact. Both are about lies, fantasy, self-delusion . . . the latter is one of the most inventive and sustained theatrical jokes of the century. . . . Even when one is familiar with the basic idea . . . one still can't help admiring the way Shaffer builds on the conceit. . . . One can even forgive Shaffer for rubbing in the point that it's really a Hellsa-poppin King Lear proving that only in darkness do we really see.

Michael Billington, *The Guardian,* 29 June 1976

There must be somewhere dark backstage at Chichester, an airing cupboard or a coal hole perhaps, where the actors withdraw for five minutes to train their eyes before they come on. . . . It is a brilliant supposition for a farce, a plotful of mistaken identities at a stroke. Derek Jacobi . . . tests the floor with little pats of his outstretched leg like a crab on a rock. Louise Purnell as his debbie girl, who keeps her high heels on — isn't one's first instinct in the dark to take them off? — walks about with her wrists braced against the air as though it were the door of a strong room. . . . But there is something else in all games with darkness that might have been developed here, something hallucinatory and out of joint that could have made the play much more startling and touching than it is about people whose usual links with one another have suddenly become damaged and suspect. *Black Comedy* would have lost no comedy if it had had the nerve to be more black; as it is, the play seemed a blinding idea not very boldly pursued.

There is a sign of its bland temperament in the fact that the physical techniques eliminate the sick fear implicit in moving in the dark. . . . The characters very seldom do anything arrestingly human in the dark; they don't yawn in a lover's face, for instance, or smell themselves, or stroke their own limbs for reassurance, or say something with an expression that they haven't bothered to match to the remark.

Obviously it is a production that could do with months of improvising rehearsal. The actor who has driven furthest so far is Albert Finney as the queer neighbour. His movements and expressions elaborate a reaction to the dark that is absolutely particular. . . . His limbs are very funny, and furious. So are Maggie Smith's curling gorilla toes before she swings into an inspired bitch's invention in the voice of an imaginary daily who reports that the deb, Maggie Smith's replacement, is at the bottom of the young master's heap. The engine of the plot is at its best here.

Penelope Gilliatt, *The Observer,* 1 Aug. 1965; reprinted in
Unholy Fools (London and New York, 1973), p. 191-2

The action requires split-second timing and steely nerves on the part of the actors not to flinch noticeably just before they fall downstairs or make painful contact with some to them invisible obstacle. As a piece of sheer theatrical machinery the play is impeccable, as brilliant as anything Shaffer has ever done. And almost indestructible: even in a far less than perfect production the structure carries the play. . . .

Inevitably there are points of connection with his other plays, ideas that carry over. The colonel in *Black Comedy* suggests a more comic re-examination of Stanley in *Five Finger Exercise.* And Bob's remarks in *The Private Ear* about the beauty of hands and people's inability to recognize even their own because they have never really looked at them are reflected vividly in the 'kinky game' Clea devises of guess-the-hand in *Black Comedy,* which gives rise incidentally to a moment of strange resonance when Harold, of all people, proves instantly able to recognize Brindsley's hand in the dark (is it possible that this figure of fun is, under it all, the only character able to step far enough out of his farcical context to have some real intense feeling about someone else?). . . . In the room, Clea's 'magic dark room, where everything happens the wrong way round', a surprising amount of light is after all shed on a surprising collection of characters.

John Russell Taylor, *Peter Shaffer* (Longman, 1974), p. 22-3

When the Chinese [pretend to be duelling in the dark] it becomes a small but infinitely refined form of art. Mr. Shaffer has elected for pratfalls, easy boffs, and every trick Sliding Billy Watson left behind in the stable. . . . Miss Redgrave, who normally stands as though one leg had been broken off and then carelessly propped back into place, takes that steeply-pitched staircase like a cater-pillar in panic, an impression that is reinforced by the jungle fronds of line-gags from having to work too hard. Your joy in the exercise will depend upon the depth of your appetite for more and more of the same.

Walter Kerr, *New York Times,* 13 Feb. 1967

White Liars

Play in one act.
First New York production (entitled *White Lies,* with *Black Comedy*): Ethel Barrymore Th., 12 Feb. 1967 (dir. John Dexter; with Geraldine Page as Sophie, Donald Madden as

Frank, and Michael Crawford as Tom).

First London production (with *Black Comedy*): Lyric Th.,
21 Feb. 1968 (dir. Peter Wood; with Dorothy Reynolds as
Sophie, James Bolam as Frank, and Ian McKellen as Tom);
revised version, Shaw Th., 28 June 1976 (dir. Paul Giovanni;
with Timothy Dalton as Tom and Maggie Fitzgibbon as
Sophie).

Published: in *Plays and Players,* April, 1966; as *Black Comedy,
including White Lies,* New York: Stein and Day, 1967. *Revised
versions:* as *White Liars,* London: Samuel French, 1967;
London: Hamish Hamilton, 1968; as 'a revised version
presented at the Shaw Theatre, 1976', London and New York:
French, 1976; in *Four Plays* (Penguin, 1981); and in *Collected
Plays. White Liars* was revised three times, and at least two of
the revisions were extensive. The synopsis that follows is a
summary of the final version, as published in *Collected Plays*.)

*'White Liars' is the name of a rock group touring in a small
English coastal town. The lead singer, Tom, and the manager,
Frank, enter the parlour of 'Baroness Lemberg' to have their
fortunes told. Frank, who goes first, offers the Baroness a bribe
to warn his singer friend away from the girl he fears he is losing
to Tom. The fortune-teller agrees, but the plan backfires when
the 'facts' of Tom's life, which Frank has supplied, turn out to be
lies which Tom has fabricated in order to give himself the working-
class past he thinks rock stars need. But Frank, too, has lied in
his desperate attempt to keep Tom as his own lover. The final
layer of 'white lies' is revealed as we learn that Sophie's own
aristocratic past is also sheer pretence.*

To precede [*Black Comedy*] I wrote a companion piece, *White
Lies.* Geraldine Page was characteristically sensitive in this play
about a fortune-teller sitting alone on a rotting English pier in a
rotten English summer. But I am afraid that I did not manage to
get it quite right. The dramatic pulse was too low, and the work
came out a little mechanically. A rewritten version entitled *The
White Liars* was subsequently done in England, very cleverly
directed by Peter Wood, with Ian McKellen as the pop singer.
This was better, though it was marred by an offstage tape representing the voice of Sophie's Greek lover. Only in a third version
(*White Liars*), directed at London's Shaw Theatre by Paul

Giovanni, did I feel the play finally work for me. . . . One day I should like to see a film of this tale. I suspect that its sea-misted atmosphere of illusion would suit the screen very well.

Shaffer, 'Preface' to *Collected Plays,* p. xiii

Neither [*White Lies* nor *The White Liars*] is very satisfactory; the most striking change between the two is the addition of the tape-recorded voice of the old seaside fortune-teller's long-lost Greek lover, which haunts her dreams. All the characters are telling lies, mostly to themselves. The fortune-teller is a middle-European Jew pretending to be a baroness and trying to force a similar fantasy (in tape-recorded flashback) on her lover. . . . The speech in which Tom, the pop-star, lays his cards on the table, is a great set-piece for an actor, but otherwise *The White Liars* is the feeblest piece by Shaffer to remain in circulation

John Russell Taylor, *Peter Shaffer* (Longman, 1974), p. 23-4

We are, in *White Lies,* to have a lesson in truth and falsehood in the very lair of chicanery. . . . Miss Page, adding to a list of fine stage portraits, is at her very best. Sophie is a strange and complex creature, a fraud herself as well as dealing in fraud. She is histrionic and subtle, flamboyant and shy, and it is she who tells her own fortune and finds her own truth. It is a splendid and unusual piece of work.

Richard P. Cooke, *Wall Street Journal,* 14 Feb. 1967

[Geraldine Page] is a down-at-the-heels fortune teller, philosophically morose in a deep black wig, rattling around all by her lonesome in a flat with a fractured ceiling, shredded draperies, and the biggest, busiest cupboard for housing what-nots. . . . The situation is arresting; it doubles back on itself neatly with the arrival of the patsy (Mr. Crawford), and then, I am sorry to say, it stops right where it is and turns into a little homily consisting mostly of Advice to the Loveless. It seems that we constantly tell lies to ourselves, whether we are fortune-tellers or not, in order to avoid love. The eyes of love make us see what we are, and that scares us. The last notion, which is not bad as such notions go, is unfortunately not dramatized, it is simply spelled out by Miss Page as mother-confessor.

Walter Kerr, *New York Times,* 13 Feb. 1967

A curious, slight, old-fashioned play. . . . By old-fashioned, of course, I do not mean basic well-made, like, say, *Five Finger Exercise* or *The Public Eye* . . . rather this is written in an ornate style, overloaded with words (many of them not necessary, since the author's meaning is conveyed perfectly well without them), and garnished with tiresome devices like ghostly voices off-stage. . . . Maybe a more substantial piece could carry all the machinery, but *The White Liars* is, or should be, essentially fast-moving and lightweight. Its subject is the favourite Pirandellian one of masks and faces, different worlds of illusion impinging for a few moments on each other, and the relativity of truth.

John Russell Taylor, *Plays and Players,* May 1968, p. 26

White Liars [is] professedly rewritten since its first London appearance. The most interesting addition, in view of the long line of male attachments in Mr. Shaffer's plays, is the explicit acknowledgement that this one really is homosexual. The most valuable subtraction is the disembodied voice with which the fortune-telling Baroness, who governs the play, was wont to hold interminable conversations. . . .

Mr. Shaffer seems more optimistic than O'Neill about man's capacity to survive the death of his illusions, which is cheering, but perhaps a dramatist needs to treat this theme at four hours' length if he is to quell our desire to know what else might be new. The play suffers, like many of Mr. Shaffer's, from its failure to find a believable idiom, especially for its young; Timothy Dalton as the singer is wet, but he is not helped by his author or by Mr. Giovanni, who lowers the lights on him and leaves him to soliloquize.

Robert Cushman, *The Observer,* 4 July 1976

Even with its internal flashbacks excised and its homosexual undercurrents spelt out, the prefatory *White Liars* remains an obstinately laborious work. . . . The trouble is it could just as easily be a short story as a play; and the production doesn't help by breaking the naturalistic convention and having Timothy Dalton's singer address the audience as if they were a public meeting.

Michael Billington, *The Guardian,* 29 June 1976

Only in *White Lies,* one of Shaffer's less notable efforts, is there a female protagonist. While she achieves a moral victory in that she sees and tells the truth in the end, she is forced to return her fortune-telling fee to the belligerent male antagonist and thereby faces an ethical defeat.

Ralph S. Carlson, 'Peter Shaffer', *Critical Survey of Drama,*
IV (New Jersey: Salem Press, 1985), p. 1680

Shrivings

Play in three acts.
First London production (as *The Battle of Shrivings*): Lyric Th.,
  5 Feb. 1970 (dir. Peter Hall; with John Gielgud as Gideon,
  Patrick Magee as Mark, and Wendy Hiller as Enid); *revised
  version:* Th. Royal, York, 26 Nov. 1975 (dir. Mervyn Willis;
  with Donald Palmer as Gideon and Peter Schofield as Mark).
Published (revised version): London: André Deutsch, 1974; in
  Equus and Shrivings (New York: Atheneum, 1974); in *Three
  Plays* (Penguin, 1976); and in *Collected Plays,* 1982. (*Shrivings*
  was revised extensively after the London production before its
  publication, and the original version was never published. The
  italicized synopsis below is of the printed version; the first
  extract in roman type describes the original version,
  The Battle of Shrivings, as produced in London.)

*Shrivings is the estate of Sir Gideon Petrie, an elderly English
pacifist. Sir Gideon has turned the estate, whose name suggests
an obvious place of confession, into a retreat 'for kids on their
way someplace'. But only four inhabitants are present during
the weekend of the play: the world-renowned pacifist himself, a
young American girl who is his secretary and disciple, an eminent
visiting poet who is a former student of Petrie's, and the poet's
son, who has more or less taken up residence there. . . . The play
poses a searing challenge by the poet, Mark, a compulsive alcoholic
cynic, to the rational idealism of the pacifist and the young girl.
Every pacifist, on or off stage, is sure to be asked, 'How far
would you go before resorting to violence? Would you allow
yourself to be crucified? Would you allow your loved ones to be
tortured? raped?' And the pacifist, if he is honest, must answer, 'I
won't know until I have met the test.' The 'battle' at Shrivings is
a conscious attempt on Mark's part to move Sir Gideon to*

violence. If Mark fails, he has promised to return to the humanistic philosophy of his former mentor. To achieve his end Mark blatantly plays on sexual drives and parental jealousy. He manages to be thoroughly obnoxious. Before the weekend is out he provokes Sir Gideon to slap the face of the American girl.

> Warren Sylvester Smith, 'Peter Shaffer', in *Dictionary of Literary Biography*, XIII p. 461

Shrivings is the name of Sir Gideon Petrie's home in the Cotswolds, the spartan, former medieval convent in which the 67-year-old liberal humanist philosopher (John Gielgud) lives a celibate, vegetarian idealistic existence with his self-effacing wife Enid (Wendy Hiller), his naively adoring American secretary Lois (Dorothy Lyman), and David (Martin Shaw), Cambridge dropout son of his onetime pupil and friend, the expatriate poet Mark Askelon (Patrick Magee).

'Shrivings', in the sense of 'confession' and 'penance,' is also the name of the game that's played there one April weekend when Mark returns from his exile in Corfu to receive with Gideon 'a joint award for humane letters'. The game is a literal one in two ways. Firstly, Mark challenges Gideon to demonstrate his pacifist principles by refraining from ejecting him whatever he might do before Sunday midnight; the conditions are that neither party will reveal to the others what is afoot, and that if Gideon succeeds, then Mark will return to the humanist fold, persuaded that such forbearance is possible. Secondly, in the course of the weekend Mark employs a series of cruel strategies to expose the illusions of Enid, Lois, and David, and undermine their faith in 'the first Pope of reason' who has turned his home into 'a cathedral of rational humanism'.

> Philip French, *Plays and Players,* March 1970, p. 20

I invested more sheer effort into this play than any other. It is really covered with the fingermarks of struggle. . . . Neither the critics nor the public took to the play at all, and it was withdrawn after a bare two months.

I was deeply depressed by the failure of this piece and by the derisory quality of the notices which greeted it. The work had meant a great deal to me. . . . However, after the pain of dismissal finally abated, I came to acknowledge a certain justness in the verdict — though none at all in the palpable pleasure with which it had been delivered. It seemed to me, on reflection, that there was a danger in my work of theme dictating event, and that a strong impulse to compose rhetorical dialectic was beginning to freeze my characters into theoretical attitudes.

Peter Shaffer, 'Preface' to *Collected Plays,* p. xiv.

For myself, the more I saw *The Battle of Shrivings* performed, the more I wanted to change it. I do not mean that I just wanted to make it work. 'Working,' in the sense intended by many theatrical professionals, far too often simply means effectiveness purchased at the price of any ambiguous insight, or of any qualifying perception not immediately accessible to a dozing audience sullenly suspicious of language. Other plays of mine had relied for their completion on elaborate stretches of physical action: in this one I wanted the electricity to be sparked almost exclusively from the spoken words. . . .

I suspected that the intransigence of the argument had been blunted by an almost conventional turn it had taken, toward the end, into domestic bickering. Certain furious passages between the husband and the wife had been undeniably useful in humanizing action otherwise largely concerned with debate, but I wondered whether fundamentally they had not constituted an easy way around the rigorous path which the piece should properly have followed. The first thing I did, when I started to rewrite, was to remove altogether the character of Enid Petrie, the pacifist's unhappy wife, thereby changing a quintet into a quartet.

Obviously the horror of this story, in any version of it, has to be Gideon's lapse into violence after so many years of self-restraint. But with Enid removed, a more dramatically interesting target for the pacifist's blow instantly appeared: Lois, his idealistic and worshipping young secretary. An assault on a committed girl seemed to me in this situation even more appalling than one on an aggrieved wife. The fact that the girl was also an American clinched the matter for me.

Shrivings has always been an 'American' play. I associate it most strongly with sojourns in New York City in 1968 and 1969. The encounter between Mark and Gideon naturally sprang out of a division of feeling in myself, but it was charged with the violence of this angry city during one of her angriest times, when streets were choked with raging protesters against the Vietnam War, newspapers were filled with the killings at Kent State University, and there drifted through our midst the fantastic army of Flower People, now already turned into ghosts. . . .

As a foreigner in America, I became so possessed by the fever of that time, and the baffling contradictions it set off in my head. . . . Man squeezed like a nut between an ideal choice and a practical one, and cracked in bits by either, is scarcely a novel image; yet the discovering of it for oneself, the coming to any sort of awareness of tragic ambiguity, must always be new and painful. . . .

English dramatic taste rather deplores the large theme, largely broached: it tends to prefer — sometimes with good sense, but often with a really dangerous fear of grossness — the minute fragment, minutely observed. I am not saying that I did the job (or have redone it) well. I simply reflect that had I remained a constant Londoner during that period, I doubt if I would have done it at all.

Shaffer, 'A Note on the Play, 1974', reprinted in
Collected Plays, p. 315-18.

In his rewriting of the play for the published text Shaffer has certainly made it more consistent, and intensified its overall gesture. . . . Recognizing perhaps that one of the play's major flaws was its uncertain hovering between naturalism and a more extravagant rhetorical style, Shaffer has chosen in the reworking to key it up rather than play it down. Gideon becomes less of the uninvolved sage, more believably a man who has fought and is still fighting a battle with emotions which he intellectually rejects. Even the already extravagant character of Mark has been keyed up somewhat, so that one senses his torment, from which his destructive urges arise, as more genuine, that he is in fact much less in control of what he says and does to prove his point than seemed to be the case in the first version. His son David remains rather a sympathetic cypher, but even he is less cool than he was, more emotional, to the point that one can believe that Mark's announcement that his mother was a whore and that David is not his son (a lie, of course, as David recognizes even at the time) could have a traumatic effect on him.

The effect of the play . . . has been moved further from state-ment . . . towards a different dimension of psychological truth . . . It is hard to know how the new version would play on stage — it would need a very careful and precise choice of style for its production and playing — but at any rate to read and imagine on the stage of one's own mind it is far more satisfactory.

John Russell Taylor, *Peter Shaffer,* p. 26.

Peter Shaffer's new play, *The Battle of Shrivings,* is long, too long for its own good. It is witty, but not always quite witty enough. But it is serious and honourable and the occasion for some strong, fine acting in Peter Hall's production. There are large parts of it which Shaw would not have at all disdained to write. . . . The early acts of battle are extremely entertaining: Sir John Gielgud, thin-lipped and apparently invulnerable; Patrick Magee, in a gorgeously rich, devilish, and gleeful part, slowly undermining the 'saint'. The flaw in the pacifist argument? We see it like a chink which widens all the time. In the end, violence takes place on more than one level – this I mean literally: while scenes of appalling domestic candour, like those one finds in Albee, strip the cocoon of lies and self-deceit away from the sage and his loveless wife, the wicked old enemy lies tippling and eavesdropping in a guest room above. In the last scenes there is antiphonal confession and despair going from room to room. At the last, the positions are almost exactly reversed: the saint is in despair, the destroyer is life-affirming.

Philip Hope-Wallace, *The Guardian,* 6 Feb. 1970

Most of the first act goes Sir Gideon's way, and most of the second the mad poet's; but since the antithesis of the latter set against the thesis of the former proves to be just as invalid in its premises, I could see no point in staying to see the synthesis, if one emerged in the final hour. For what it's worth, this is the first time I have departed early from a play so evidently, honourably serious in intention: but this was an utterly, unbelievably botched piece of work – not even worth the trouble of engaging oneself *against,* like *US* [the RSC play about the Vietnam War], and I was so bored by the sixth-form level of the squabbling that I could bear no more. That a play about a liberal philosopher said to have led the first sit-down in Parliament Square should have opened in the week of Bertrand Russell's death only highlighted the puerile bad taste of the affair.

Simon Trussler, *Tribune,* 27 Feb. 1970

The idea of combining in one confrontation Bertrand Russell's tragi-comic attempts at befriending T.S. Eliot and D.H. Lawrence is a brilliant one, but Shaffer simply isn't equipped to cope with its implications. No philosopher would step for a second into the trap of arguing the question of man's animal nature on the same ground as a programme of moral exhortation. Or if he did, it would be by forcing his opponent to recognize that his definition of man as an aggressive beast is a persuasive one, designed to underpin an alternative system of 'animal' ethics. The real Russell would have blown Mark Askelon out of Shrivings' Gothic windows with one cawing, derisive blast of logical analysis.

Instead, he's played by John Gielgud as a figure of tremulous nobility obviously destined to shatter into fragments of phoney-ness. Too sweet-natured to be true, he crumples at the first on-slaught of manufactured malevolence, allowing the demonstration of his shortcomings to bring down the whole argument for trying to overcome them.

Ronald Bryden, 'Echoes of Russell', *The Observer,* 8 Feb. 1970

Shrivings is a Shaw play without Shaw. Where the master could have whirled the philosopher to triumph in a blaze of intellectual toughness and passion, Shaffer slips the poet the victory with too little of either. In the end, Sir Gideon is forced to throw out everything except Askelon in a battle that is not so much pitched as rigged. Gielgud lends the part a tremulous, blinking dignity, but he can only play it the way Shaffer wrote it: as the milque-toast of human kindness. Like the devil, the devil's advocate has all the best lines, even if many of them are overwrought and over-writ. It is Magee's poet — haranguing, seducing, at once flailing out with and wincing from his own lash — who jolts the play occasion-ally into the corrosive credibility it ought to sustain throughout.
Time, 30 Mar. 1970, p. 77

Seldom have I felt so totally out of step with my fellow critics as over the near-unanimous damnation of Peter Shaffer's *The Battle of Shrivings* at the Lyric. . . . What no-one said was that here was an elegant, exultant, erudite, civilized, witty, unashamedly theatrical, and hence unfashionable play. For the feeling around the West End at the moment, it would seem, is that it's some-how improper for a playwright to write deliberately and openly for his chosen medium; the very word 'theatrical' is no longer a term of approbation and Mr. Shaffer's sin was to create charac-ters larger than life who could then fight the Man versus God battle on a truly gigantic scale in the strongest play of familiar ideas to have hit London in a long time.
Sheridan Morley, *The Tatler,* reprinted in *Review Copies* (Robson, 1975), p. 22-3

Peter Shaffer's ferocious and despairing play was first performed in London, under a slightly different title, in 1970. . . Dissatisfied with its format, the author withdrew it and rewrote extensively; the result is the powerful, exquisitely agonizing, work at York Theatre Royal — dramatic acupuncture where the practitioner often lets his hand slip to pin nerve against bone. . . .

Considering that it is overtly a 'message' play, *Shrivings* is as compulsive as a thriller: an exciting and dangerous entertainment. One flaw is perhaps that the battle of ideologies is mismatched. One sympathizes with the poet faced with the smug people and their glib 'peace' greeting. . . . And the author could not, I'm sure, have wished for a better Askelon than Peter Schofield, a bloated passionate animal who goes screaming with rage and pain into the void.

Stephen Dixon, *The Guardian,* 27 Nov. 1975

Equus

Play in two acts.

First London production: Old Vic Th., 26 July 1973 (dir. John Dexter; with Alec McGowen as Martin Dysart, Peter Firth as Alan Strang, and Gillian Burge as Hesther Salomon); transferred to the Albery Th., 20 Apr. 1976 (with Colin Blakely as Dysart and Gerry Sundquist as Alan).

First New York production: Plymouth Th., 24 Oct. 1974 (dir. John Dexter, with Anthony Hopkins as Dysart, Peter Firth as Alan, and Marian Seldes as Hesther).

Film version: screenplay by Shaffer, 1977 (dir. Sidney Lumet; with Richard Burton as Dysart and Peter Firth as Alan).

Published: London: André Deutsch, 1973; in *Equus and Shrivings* (New York: Atheneum, 1974); London: Samuel French, 1974; New York: Avon, 1975; in *Three Plays* (Penguin, 1976); in *Collected Plays,* 1982; ed. T.S. Pearce, with a personal essay by Shaffer, London: Longman, 1983.

Equus *intertwines two stories: that of a seventeen-year-old boy, Alan Strang, who has been remitted to a psychiatric hospital after he blinded six horses with a metal spike; and that of his psychiatrist, Martin Dysart, who seeks to uncover the causes of Alan's bizarre crime, and for whom the case becomes a catalyst for his own doubts about his professional and personal life. Alan has* been referred to Dysart by Hesther Salomon, a compassionate magistrate who serves as Dysart's confidante in the play. The play is set in a square of wood which 'resembles a railed boxing ring'. Wooden benches placed within and outside the square accommodate the actors, who 'get up to perform their scenes, and return when they are done to their places around the set. They are witnesses, assistants – and especially a Chorus'. Martin Dysart narrates the play, beginning with the image of the boy embracing a horse. Then, in the 21 scenes of Act One and the 14 of Act Two, he recounts the story of his treatment of Alan through therapy, hypnosis, and a phony 'truth drug' – all leading Alan to 'abreact' or relive the events leading to the cruel act. Dysart's interviews with Alan's parents reveal the mother as middle-class and fervently religious, while the father, a printer by trade, is an atheist and socialist, proud of his lower-class background. Except for forbidding Alan to watch television (which his mother secretly allowed), he has communicated little with his son. Three events stand out. First, Alan remembers his first ride on a horse as a child, a wonderful and sexually stimulating gallop, abruptly ended by his father, who pulled him roughly from the stranger's horse – not, however, before Alan sensed the horse 'speaking' to him. Second, encouraged by his mother's reading passages about horses from the Bible, Alan replaced a picture of the suffering Jesus, which his father had torn from his bedroom wall, with a picture of a horse ('absolutely head on ... It comes out all eyes.') Finally, the father admits to having accidentally observed his son engaged in a ritual of worship before the picture, culminating in self-flagellation. Dysart pieces these clues together to conclude that Alan has created his own primitive religion based on the horse-cum-god Equus. Having obtained work at a stable, Alan has secretly taken the horses out at night. In the final scene of Act One, he recreates his naked ride in wild ecstasy as he seeks to become one with his animal god (the horses are portrayed by actors wearing wire horse masks and metal hooves). As Dysart exposes the layers of Alan's psyche, he becomes increasingly reluctant to make the boy conform to the 'normal' world, which the psychiatrist characterizes as plastic and shrunken, without worship. He sees his own life as sterile and passionless and comes to envy Alan's unique but passionate psychosis. He dreams repeatedly of himself as a priest in ancient

*Greece carving up children, taking from them essential organs as a
sacrifice to the god 'Normal'. The second act uncovers the rest of
the mystery. In Alan's final scenes of 'abreaction' he attempts, unsuccessfully, a sexual relationship with Jill, his co-worker at the
stable. The all-seeing Equus is a jealous god who allows no infidelity
of human flesh. After Jill has left the stable, Alan, in a frenzy of
guilt and failure, puts out the horses' eyes. At the conclusion of
this emotional scene, Dysart is left with the naked, sedated boy,
the haunting image of Equus, and his agonizing doubts.*

The actors [playing horses] wear tracksuits of chestnut velvet. On
their feet are light strutted hooves, about four inches high, set on
metal horseshoes. On their hands are gloves of the same colour.
On their heads are tough masks made of alternating bands of
silver wire and leather; their eyes are outlined by leather blinkers.
The actors' own heads are seen beneath them: no attempts should
be made to conceal them.

Any literalism which could suggest the cosy familiarity of a
domestic animal — or worse, a pantomime horse — should be
avoided. The actors should never crouch on all fours, or even
bend forward. They must always — except on the one occasion
where Nugget is ridden — stand upright, as if the body of the
horse extended invisibly behind them. Animal effect must be
created entirely mimetically, through the use of legs, knees, neck,
face, and the turn of the head which can move the mask above it
through all the gestures of equine wariness and pride. Great care
must also be taken that the masks are put on before the audience
with very precise timing — the actors watching each other, so that
the masking has an exact and ceremonial effect.

Shaffer, *Collected Plays*, p. 400

The tale told to me by my friend James Mossman of the BBC . . .
was not remotely the one I told the audience. In the version
which he briefly referred to . . . the boy was the son of very
repressive and religious eccentrics; he had been seduced by a girl
on the floor of the stable; he had blinded the animals in a panic
to erase the memory of his sin and to prevent them from bearing
witness to it before his parents. This climax, allegedly told to
Mossman by a magistrate, I found absolutely impossible to write.
There was no way in which a boy's first satisfactory sexual
encounter could lead on stage to such horrific violence — unless it

had not been satisfactory at all. Unless, that is, the presence of the horses had directly prevented that satisfaction. And why would that be − unless the horses themselves were the focus of some deep attachment which consummation with the girl would betray? This disturbing thought vitalized the story for me and took hold of my mind. I set about writing a play of obsession, possibly unshareable in its nature by very many people and probably shocking to them as well. . . . I think I had not sufficiently realized when I began *Equus* how deeply the levelling and limiting of the human psyche by the cult of a narrowly defined Normality is a common preoccupation of our time.

Shaffer, 'Preface' to *Collected Plays,* p. xiv

Equus is surely, among other things, the name one individual gives to his impulse for worship. I think that is the telegrammic statement about *Equus.* And like all gods of that kind, like almost all gods I've ever heard of, it is an ambiguous presence − both conquering and submissive, both judging and accusing on the one hand and accepting and gentle on the other. He wears a double aspect, and this double aspect is very important, and paralleled when Dr. Dysart, the psychiatrist, reflects on the normal. . . . The psychiatrist's perception of what the word 'normal' means parallels the ambiguous nature of his god Equus in the mind of the boy. . . .

The boy has found, no matter how strange the ritual is − against a background of rather dreary and colourless provincial life, working with not much to look forward to in an electrical and kitchenware shop, with an unimaginative but kindly father and an unimaginative but kindly mother (they're much the same although one happens to believe in God and one does not), and no doubt surrounded by four- and six-lane highways going to the guts of cities, surrounded by concrete eggboxes and the dreary paraphernalia of modern life − his own source of ecstasy. Dysart has no choice but to remove that from him, with very little guarantee that he'll be able to find anything to put in its place. . . .

Jung, when talking about neurosis said, 'Neurosis is an escape from legitimate pain'. Until I read that, I hadn't quite been aware that there *was* such a thing as legitimate pain. I think Jung is one of the greatest minds of the twentieth century. . . . Jung is so intensely grounded in myth.

Most people do not realize − and by 'realize' I mean they do not feel intensely, from day to day, in any way that truly affects them − that we did not begin the world, that we are repositories, walking encyclopedias, of all human experience, that we contain within us, within our heads and without our genes, the whole of human history. This sounds abstract and irrelevant to most people who just want to get on with living; but the more one comes to realize that the cells of one's brain contain endless archetypal images that stretch back beyong the Stone Age, the more one can come to an immense and important sense of who one is, for himself, instead of just a little worried package of responses and reflexes, sexual drives and frustrations. Jung is the poet of psychiatry.

Shaffer, Vogue, Feb. 1975, p. 136, 192

The horse is a warm, beautiful, proud, and ravishing object. . . . People can understand boys' sexual interest in girls, and, today, boys in boys, but boys with horses? Yet horses quite clearly have a sexual identity. They are born savage and powerful — they could stamp us to death — but they are also submissive. At one point in the play there is an immense orgiastic release. The boy says to the horse, 'Bear me away', which is what a lot of religious poets say to God in their poetry. This particular god is capable of carrying him away. . . . It gave me a feeling of chaos inside. I found it very difficult to write. I experimented with onomatopeia, with keeping the frenzy verbal, but there must be a moment when the visual takes over.

Shaffer, interviewed by Mel Gussow, New York Times,
24 Oct. 1974, p. 50

The really startling thing about the reception accorded to Equus here was that the sea-change was complete. To sum it up as a joke, in England the play was found shocking because it seemed cruel to horses, in America because it seemed cruel to psychiatrists. . . . The first preview of Equus in New York therefore was electrifying to me because I suddenly realized that the play was turning into something completely different before my very eyes. Every remark which could be construed in any way as anti-psychiatric fed the audience's apparent communal fantasy of enjoying revenge on its doctors. They seemed almost to want to hear the profession discredited. They clapped and laughed heartily at lines which in London had been spoken in complete silence. This was really very startling to me, and highly revealing about the differences in assumption in our two cultures.

Shaffer, Dramatists Guild Quarterly, Spring 1980, p. 30

The boy in *Equus* grew out of a feeling that for a lot of people in suburban England life has gone flat. It is what one heard on all sides — 'England is not what it used to be, life is savourless, people feel frustrated by its relentless prosaicism.'

Shaffer, interviewed by Brian Connell,
The Times, 28 Apr. 1980

The play has been subject to a vast amount of commentary and misuse: a few doctors declaring it a madman's charter; some do-your-own-thingers using it as a means to justify every kind of human aberration. For me it is a deeply erotic play, and also one of tragic conflict. Tragedy obviously does not lie in a conflict of Right and Wrong, but in a collision between two different kinds of Right: in this case, surely, between Dysart's professional obligation to treat a terrified boy who has committed a dreadful crime, and Alan's passionate capacity for worship. . . . Dysart has to do what he does. . . . Yet in proceeding by his best and honourable lights, the doctor cannot but know that he is in some clear sense the destroyer of a passion he must forever, and rightly, envy.

Shaffer, 'A Personal Essay', in *Equus,* ed. T.S. Pearse
(Longman, 1983), p. viii-ix

Within three years . . . *Equus* has laid claim to the title of the most quickly successful serious British play ever. . . . When John Dexter's National Theatre production officially reaches the West End, opening at the Albery Theatre . . . *Equus* will already probably have been seen in half the countries of the developed world. . . . In Britain there have been 131 performances in two sequences at the Old Vic, and productions in 15 regional centres — this latter figure so low only because the rights were released for no more than a few months before the National reclaimed them. Even Australia has done better than that: the play has been round the major theatre chains in the cities, and right round the outback too. . . .

What happens in the States still matters above all, and there the play is said to have broken every box-office record in practically every theatre where it has been presented. The other leading role, of the psychiatrist, created by Alec McCowen at the Old Vic, has been played by Anthony Hopkins, Anthony Perkins, and Richard Burton among others. On Broadway, where Dexter's production has been running for nearly two years (currently with Burton), it became the first play ever to win all the New York theatre awards, including the Tony for best play and best director. . . .

If you are one of those who find other people's enthusiasms a bit boring, you will be relieved to hear that the play was quite slow to pick up in Germany, possibly because the first production was on the weak side. . . . But from Israel to Venezuela, Iceland to Japan, there seems to be a most peculiar unanimity. They went wild in South Africa, where Dai Bradley moved on from the National's second run to play the part of the boy. In France, where there has been much competition between theatres, the play is due to open soon, co-directed by Jean-Louis Barrault and Dexter.

Christopher Ford, 'The *Equus* Stampede',
The Guardian, 20 Apr. 1976

The salient feature of the play's craft is its construction. The stage is as bare as a surgical arena. Around it are several tiers of seats on which student members of the audience are placed, as if observing a lecture demonstration. On the left and right sides, close to the observers, are seated the play's characters; they leave their positions only when the script calls upon them to enact their parts in the drama. A battery of powerful lights shine down on the platform to lend the proceedings an atmosphere of scientific precision. Horses play a crucial role in the story; actors are clearly visible within the horses' heads of gilt metal, and their hooves of similar material not only give them great height but contribute an ominous effect by the clatter they make on the burnished wood floor.

Very few props are employed; the scenic style is generally non-realistic except, curiously enough, when a boy and girl of the play set about to make love, at which time they are seen in total nudity. While the overall impression is one of severe functionalism, an air of spectacle, of *theatre,* obtains in which dramatist, actors, and director display their skills with gratifying aplomb.

Harold Clurman, *The Nation,* 16 Nov. 1974, p. 506

It's like a kind of perfect play. It's got all the theatrical ingredients. There's a big acting problem, because it's very passionate but the passion has to be controlled in a surgical way. There are two very conflicting emotions in the part which have to be polarized. . . . In a way [the part of Pizarro in *Royal Hunt of the Sun*] was very like this — people trying to do the right thing, but the two protagonists in the end somehow destroying each other. I think Peter is one writer who manages to get right to the edge of experience. I don't know what it's like out in the audience, watching *Equus,* but when you're playing it you can feel this atmosphere all around you . . . in the dark. He manages to evoke the gods.

Colin Blakely (Dysart), quoted by Christopher Ford,
The Guardian, 20 Apr. 1976

Dysart is no ordinary psychiatrist. He's an eccentric, a driven, isolated man. . . . He's someone who can articulate very well on the special privacy of pain. As a result, he's always questioning. . . . To me Dysart, who's at first just plain curious about the boy, gets sucked into his patient's torment almost against his will. He envies the boy for his passion; in the end it becomes his own.

Richard Burton, interviewed by Patricia Bosworth,
New York Times, 4 Apr. 1976, Sec. 2, p. 10

[Burton's] — more than any of his predecessors — is unabashedly a star performance. It starts from the posture — he stands at the middle of the world, and when he muses, he does so with a kind of interior poetry. He is not one's idea of a man who would be a moderately failed psychiatrist . . . yet somehow his larger-than-life approach works.

Clive Barnes, *New York Times,* 27 Feb. 1976, p. 16

I used to have nightmares about it. . . . Naturally the dreams were filled with horses. I felt emotionally disturbed. It is quite an experience to go through. In the London production I played opposite Alec McCowen as the analyst. He's a fantastic technician. He thought everything through. Acting with Tony Hopkins, here in New York, is a whole other thing. He's a more instinctive actor, so I had to change my approach a bit. I know that in order for my role to have the right kind of passion, the performance has to be very controlled, very quiet, very disciplined. Otherwise it would be imprecise. . . . Alan Strang . . . is just a mass of repressions, put there by his parents, by his fixation on religion, on sex, on horses. No wonder he cracked!

Peter Firth (Strang), interviewed by John Gruen,
New York Times, 27 Oct. 1974, Sec. 2, p. 5

As the umpire in the dramatic dialectic Martin Dysart is a naturally complex character. He was first played at the National Theatre in London with dry concern by Alec McCowen. It was a splendid performance — neat, almost finicky, yet with an undertone of suppressed feeling, a sense of despairing outrage, a special feel for futility.

The first New York Dysart, Anthony Hopkins, fleshed out the psychiatrist with more humanity. Mr. Hopkins, puzzled, good-looking, was almost pugnacious in his tenacity at reaching the truth about Alan Strang. . . . There was a certain no-nonsense air to Mr. Hopkins that was almost comforting.

Anthony Perkins, Mr. Hopkins's immediate successor in the Broadway production, somehow seemed to combine both approaches — he seemed to be somewhere in between the arid yet kindly intelligence of McCowen and the bluff eloquence of Hopkins. But the role is capable of still more interpretations — which is surely remarkable in a modern play. Currently America has two very different Dysarts — Richard Burton who is playing *Equus* on Broadway and has just picked up a Tony award for it, and Brian Bedford, who has been playing the Dysart in Boston since 18 November of last year.

Burton's Dysart comes from the Welsh bible-belt of chapels, choirs, and fiery eloquence. . . . Some of my New York colleagues have acclaimed Burton's performance as the best thing he has done on the stage . . . his Dysart is a stirring, beautiful portrayal, full of sound and fury. . . .

Mr. Bedford accepts the playwright's description of the role as 'pallid and provincial', a man despairing of his own 'timidity'. Except for a few frustrated roars of a burnt-out passion, Mr. Bedford is shabby and humorous. His suit doesn't quite fit, a ballpoint pen sticks out of his jacket pocket, and, all in all, he is flagrantly mediocre, and corrosively funny about it. This is impeccable acting.

Clive Barnes, 'The History of Mr. Dysart',
The Times, 24 Apr. 1976, p. 11

In my experience, dull, respectable middle-class homes are seldom the soil from which psychopathic violence grows. . . . Backgrounds of this kind are likely to produce joyless inhibition; but sadistic violence which is put into practice ('acted out') is more often the product of neglect, abandonment or direct parental cruelty. . . .

Anthony Storr, 'Ruling Passion', *Sunday Times,*
30 Sept. 1973, p. 29

To the psychiatrist, the boy's delusional rituals are a fascinating work of art — a sentiment which echoes R.D. Laing's once-modish sermons about respecting our patients' psychotic productions as creative acts, as higher, more authentic forms of 'truth'. . . . Perhaps in Shaffer's skilful mixture of truth, banality and pretension there is . . . something that gratifies our universal fantasies about our therapists. . . .

> Sanford Gifford, M.D., 'Psychoanalyst Says Nay to *Equus*',
> *New York Times,* 15 Dec. 1974, Sec. D, p. 1, 5

Peter Shaffer's *Equus* is sensationally good. Like *The Royal Hunt of the Sun* and *The Battle of Shrivings,* it is based on a direct confrontation between reason and instinct. Like them also, it suggests that, though organized faith is usually based on neurosis, a life without some form of worship or belief is ultimately barren. But it's a far better play than either if only because the intellectual argument and the poetic imagery are virtually indivisible. . . .

What makes the play so exciting is that it presents this argument in such bold, clear, vivid theatrical terms. From the opening image of the boy nuzzling another actor clad in skeletal horse's head and hooves, we are constantly aware of his strange passion; yet the main action takes place inside a sparse rectangular room representing the orderly world of the psychiatrist. Shaffer is also shrewd enough to make the psychiatrist a complex human figure, aware that his hunger for a pagan, primitive world is scarcely fulfilled by a three-week package tour to the Peloponnese.

> Michael Billington, *The Guardian,* 27 July 1973

If there is one thing more than another that a contemporary playwright would like to do, it is to make a myth. We feel a desperate need these days for new icons, images, clothed symbols that will help us come to terms with the 'dark cave of the psyche', the cave that thousands of years of reasoning haven't quite lighted after all. . . .

The closest I have seen a contemporary play come — it is powerfully close — to reanimating the spirit of mystery that makes the stage a place of breathless discovery rather than a classroom for rational demonstration is Peter Shaffer's remarkable *Equus*. . . .

Over-all, it is the image that stands, and is complete. The boy, with his dangerous creativity, fills one half of it, forever driven, forever blocked. The doctor fills the other, feverishly unwilling to do what he must do, doing it — only to block himself. The two fit together at unpredictable angles, like differently coloured pieces in a stained-glass window, but they fit and use up all the space that there is. Any move either makes destroys the other. Locked horns, both right, no escape. The play is perfectly proportioned to its mutual pain.

Walter Kerr, *New York Times,* 2 Sept. 1973

Equus falls into that category of worn-out whimsy wherein we are told that insanity is more desirable, admirable, or just saner than sanity. . . . *Equus* still asks us to believe that the crazed passion of a stable-boy for horses . . . is a fine and high-flown thing, a love that must be quashed because it is too grand, wild, and beautiful for the humdrum world of plodding humanity. To me, this is nonsense, and I don't for a moment believe the play's psychiatrist who is made to verbalize this bull (or horse). . . .

Next, and relatedly, the play asks us to believe that the psychiatrist who cures and 'saves' this horse worshipper and blinder diminishes him: makes him plain unpoetic, and common. . . . I particularly resent the further loading of the dice by making the psychiatrist, the spokesman for normality, an unhappily married man, his sex life with a dull and frigid wife completely atrophied, and his kicks coming from the perusal of illustrated tomes on Greek art. . . .

The play, furthermore, espouses the form of the case history, which, with the exception of the courtroom drama, is the most overworked and by now least imaginative form of theatrical offering. It is the difference between a great painting and its exploitation as a jigsaw puzzle. . . .

Lastly, we get that fashionable bitter-sweet, semi-happy ending: even if being cured is a cosmic cop-out, the boy, at least, will be cured — as if psychotherapy were such a simple matter: a little hypnosis here, a bit of abreaction there, and our hideously disturbed protagonist's mind is safely on the way to total recovery. But the final blow is the ordinariness of the play's language.

John Simon, *New York Magazine,* 11 Nov. 1974, p. 118

There live three good story-tellers in the British theatre and two of them are called Shaffer. But the neatness and the logic of these proceedings carry their own penalty. Peter Shaffer's Dr. Dysart solves his case, snaps up all the detail his author has so carefully provided, and in so doing destroys half our belief. Mr. Shaffer is such an explanatory playwright that his main charge against the psychiatrist — that he analyzes emotion out of existence — rebounds on the play itself.

Dr. Dysart does not stop at explaining his patient; he explains himself. He analyzes his marriage and berates himself for its failure; he goes on to lacerate himself for maintaining a genteel cult of the Primitive . . . instead of simply embracing it (as, in two senses, Alan has). I suppose Mr. Shaffer writes these expository passages as well as anyone could; but the play groans under them. They belong to an outworn tradition, neither realistic nor honestly stylized. These scenes are only peripheral, but there is a similar confusion at the play's centre, in the encounters between psychiatrist and patient. They are soberly set up, but when the going gets rough, and interrogation gives way to confession, we are liable to plunge into the theatricality of acted flashbacks.

Robert Cushman, *The Observer,* 29 July 1973, p. 30

On the film

When *Equus* was contracted for the movie screen, [Shaffer] made certain that he was connected with the operation (as the writer of the movie script, it turned out) to keep an eye on the project. Unfortunately, the *Equus* film brought Shaffer nothing but added grief. Despite the respected director, Sidney Lumet, and such exceptional performers as Richard Burton, Peter Firth, and Joan Plowright, the movie of *Equus* missed the mark, ending up a box-office disaster although it earned both male leads Academy Award nominations. . . . One crucial handicap to its success was a boycott supported by a national movement for animal rights. The issue of cruelty to animals was raised when Lumet insisted on simulating the blinding of the horses in ultra-realistic fashion. . . .

About the resulting film, Shaffer said: 'I wrote the script originally. Not that it did me much good, because the script I wrote was not really shot. I think . . . I did much more imaginative work than was shot. . . . I don't want to attack anybody particularly. Sidney Lumet did a very competent job. And he included me in all the time. What depressed me about the film is that it didn't have any of the images I wanted to see in it. I was very disappointed in the visual side of it. . . .

'Lumet failed in particular with those pivotal episodes when Alan Strang is abreacting. Most desperately misguided of all . . . were the shot decisions in the final stable scene. There, Strang encounters his sexuality in clinical fashion through Jill, in total, realistic nudity but without any sense of love. Alan confronts his god Equus physically — not spiritually — by realistically hacking out the horses' eyes. Absolutely none of the mystery so central to the play is retained in the movie.'

Shaffer noted that he could not bear to watch the blinding scene when it was shot, nor can he look at it even now on the screen — so painful was its crude literalism.

> C.J. Gianakaris, 'Drama into Film: the Shaffer Situation', *Modern Drama,* XXVIII (March 1985), p. 87-8, 97.

If ever there was a play that has no business being a movie, *Equus* is it. This drama . . . owed much of its three-year Broadway run to theatrical devices that cannot be reproduced on film. Strip the stagecraft away, and all that remains of *Equus* is two and a half hours of talky debate about shopworn ideas. The poor play stumbles and falls before it can break from the gate. . . . Director Lumet . . . shoots Shaffer's original stage script as is, to the point of having characters address monologues directly to the camera.

> Frank Rich, *Time,* 31 Oct. 1977, p. 48

A selection of other articles and reviews

Hélène L. Baldwin, *'Equus:* Theater of Cruelty or Theater of Sensationalism?' *West Virginia University Philological Papers,* XXV (1979), p. 118-27.

Una Chandhuri, 'The Spectator in Drama/Drama in the Spectator', *Modern Drama,* XXVII (1984), p. 281-98.

John Corbally, 'The *Equus* Ethic', *New Laurel Review,* VII, No. 11 (1977), p. 53-8.

I. Dean Ebner, 'The Double Crisis of Sexuality and Worship in Shaffer's *Equus'*, *Christianity and Literature,* XXXI, No. 2 (1982), p. 29-47.

Jules Glenn, 'Alan Strang as an Adolescent: a Discussion of Peter Shaffer's *Equus'*, *International Journal of Psychoanalytic Psychotherapy,* V (1976), p. 473-87.

Oscar Grusky, 'Equestrian Follies', *Psychology Today,* XL, Oct. 1977, p. 21-2.

Frank Lawrence, 'The *Equus* Aesthetic: the Doctor's Dilemma', *Four Quarters,* XXIX, No. 2, p. 13-18.

James Lee, *'Equus,* Round Three', *Exchange,* II (Spring 1976), p. 49-59.

Jeffrey B. Loomis, 'As Margaret Mourns: Hopkins, Goethe, and

Shaffer on Eternal Delight', *Cithara,* XXII, No. 1 (1982), p. 22-38.

Dennis Klein, 'Literary Onomastics in Peter Shaffer's *Shrivings* and *Equus', Literary Onomastic Studies,* VII (1980), p. 127-38.

Michael D. Miner, 'Grotesque Drama in the 'Seventies', *Kansas Quarterly,* XII (Fall 1980), p. 99-109.

Gene F. Plimka, 'The Existential Ritual: Peter Shaffer's *Equus', Kansas Quarterly,* XII (Fall 1980), p. 87-97.

Susan L. Schwartz, 'Symbolic Imagery and the Realm of the Psyche, *Journal of Dharma,* IX, No. 2 (1984), p. 120-31.

Julian L. Stamm, 'Peter Shaffer's *Equus* — a Psychoanalytic Exploration', *International Journal of Psychoanalytic Psychotherapy,* V (1976), p. 449-61.

Samuel Terrien, *'Equus:* Human Conflicts and the Trinity', *The Christian Century,* 18 May 1977, p. 472-6.

Neil Timm, *'Equus* as a Modern Tragedy', *West Virginia University Philological Papers,* XXV (1979), p. 128-34.

Russell Vandenbroucke, *'Equus:* Modern Myth in the Making', *Drama and Theatre,* XII (Spring 1975), p. 129-33.

Doyle W. Walls, *'Equus:* Shaffer, Nietzsche, and the Neuroses of Health', *Modern Drama,* XXIV (Sept. 1984), p. 314-23.

John Weightman, 'Christ as Man and Horse', *Encounter,* March 1975, p. 44-6.

Barry B. Witman, 'The Anger in *Equus', Modern Drama,* XXII (March 1979). p. 61-6.

Amadeus

Play in two acts.

First London production: Olivier Th., 2 Nov. 1979 (dir. Peter Hall; with Paul Scofield as Salieri and Simon Callow as Mozart); reproduced at Her Majesty's Th., 4 July 1981 (with Frank Finlay as Salieri and Richard O'Callaghan as Mozart).

First New York production: Broadhurst Th., 17 Dec. 1980 (dir. Peter Hall; with Ian McKellen as Salieri and Tim Curry as Mozart; later John Wood as Salieri and Peter Firth as Mozart).

Film version: script by Shaffer, released in US Sept. 1984, in Britain Jan. 1985 (dir. Milos Forman; with F. Murray Abraham as Salieri and Tom Hulce as Mozart).

Published: Deutsch, 1980. Substantially revised text (as played in New York and in London in 1981): New York: Harper and Row, 1981, with 'Preface' by Shaffer; Penguin, 1981; in *Collected Plays,* 1982; ed. Richard Adams, Longman Study

Text, 1984; and in *Landmarks of Modern British Theatre, II: the Seventies,* ed. Roger Cornish and Violet Ketels (Methuen, 1985). The 'film edition' (Harper and Row, 1984) contains an additional 'Introduction to the Film Edition' by Shaffer, but this is *not* the film script, which is unpublished.

The play opens with whispered gossip – at first disembodied, then voiced by the shapes of hurrying figures – about Salieri's claim to have murdered Mozart. We meet the aged Salieri, confined to a wheelchair by 1823, addressing the future about the bargain with God he made at the age of sixteen: 'Let me be a composer.' The action then moves back to the 1780s in Vienna, with the threat posed to Salieri as a court composer by the arrival in the city of the highly-praised young Mozart, whom he overhears in vulgar conversation with his fiancee Constanze. As Mozart struggles in poverty, Salieri, convinced of the sublimity of his rival's music, abandons his bargain with God and decides to destroy Mozart. In Act Two, Salieri repudiates good works, seduces his prettiest pupil, and denies a post to Mozart – who nonetheless wins the emperor's approval when he presents The Marriage of Figaro. *However, it is Salieri who becomes Kapellmeister, while Mozart declines into yet deeper poverty – his* Magic Flute *appearing, only to alienate potential friends among the masons it seems to expose. Mozart becomes obsessed with a strange figure who commands a Requiem Mass from him: then Salieri himself is transformed into this apparition. Mozart dies, Constanze beside him. Salieri returns in 1823, claims to have murdered Mozart, pronounces himself the 'Patron Saint of Mediocrities', and cuts his throat – but does not die.*

At the climax of the play *Amadeus,* in a speech unfortunately never uttered on stage for reasons of length, the composer Antonio Salieri was to have informed the audience: 'The God I acknowledge lives, for example, in bars 34 to 44 of Mozart's *Masonic Funeral Music*'. The extremity of this statement – which, incidentally, is not uttered in the film version either, because of a less verbal and more cinematic script – stirred me profoundly. It permitted my protagonist to cite specific bars of music as evidence of the presence of divinity in the world, rather than just to talk in vague, exalted terms about genius. Surely the specific is always the point in art. . . . My own apprehension of the divine is very largely aesthetic. . . . The creation of the C minor Mass or the final act of *Antony and Cleopatra* seem to me to give a point to evolution; most human activities do not. . . .

Nobody has suffered more than Mozart from sentimental misjudgment. The last century dealt with the glory of his composure by calling him 'mellifluous', as if he were really just the Fragonard of music. . . . Neither play nor picture even remotely represents a documentary life of Mozart, but both rely deliberately and delightedly on this most magical of stage conventions: a nearly absurd use of concealment to reveal emotion far from absurd.

Shaffer, The Times, 16 Jan. 1985

The grim 'messenger in grey' is entirely uncharacteristic of [Mozart's] life − yet it is the one most beloved by the early nineteenth century. It is generally accepted that in his last tormented months, when he was the victim of wretched health and an even more destructive sense of being unwanted as a composer, Mozart was visited by an ominous figure who commissioned from him, on behalf of an unnamed great patron, a Requiem Mass. Mozart in his failing state came to believe that the patron was God, and the Mass for himself. Thereafter he allegedly continued to see this messenger regarding him urgently from various corners of the city. . . .

I am greatly indebted to this legend. I have myself, in writing plays, been 'haunted' three times by apocryphal images: pictures of events which may be real or imaginary, and which either way emit an immense power. This watching figure is the latest. . . . [It] emerged more and more as I worked on *Amadeus.* It too had eyes − masked, and bent intently upon a small eighteenth-century house, in a tiny street, at night. It was a ravening figure, possessed and would-be possessing. Obviously it was born out of the legend of the grey messenger, yet for me it came to signify not merely warnings of death but worse. The picture showed Envy, glued in place like a sentinel outside the dwelling of Genius: a macabre and yet pitiable icon of consuming artistic jealousy. . . .Perhaps many plays proceed from this kind of haunting: from apocryphal images seeking their confirmation in public show. . . . The Sun God dead in his square. The Horse God dead in his stable. The God in music dying in his slum, watched by the worshipper who has destroyed him. All three pictures show the extinction of

61

divinity. Perhaps it is this which gives them all the power to haunt.

Shaffer, The Observer, 4 Nov. 1979

I tried to write a play, not history. What the play is trying to do is give an interpretation of history. But there are certain facts on which I worked. We know Mozart was broke at the end of his life. We know he was ill. We know his home was freezing. We know that he couldn't afford a fire. . . . When he died, his list of possessions was pathetically small. He *did* die in poverty.

All the elements of the play are as near to the facts as I could verify. Then I tried to work them into a dramatic climax. The confrontation between Mozart and Salieri could have happened. We *know* that Mozart took him to a performance of *The Magic Flute* and it is not unreasonable to assume that Salieri would drop in on him while he was ill to see how he was doing. . . . Salieri's way of ruining Mozart once and for all is consistent with the way the rumours went. . . .

I now look back on *Amadeus* and say 'Of course! That's what it was! Opera!' I never deliberately sat down and said I was going to compose an opera. But as I worked, I could see operatic elements. Here was an opening chorus, the whispers of the populace. Here, with the entrance of the two gossipy courtiers, was a duet. Here is a trio, and later a quintet. Salieri's monologues are the big arias. The play has the savour, the smell and taste, of an opera. Peter's production matches it.

Shaffer, quoted by Harold C. Shonberg, New York Times,
14 Dec. 1980, Sec. II, p. 1, 35

From Peter Hall's diaries

25 Jan. 1979 Peter's script is tougher, more precise, and more personal than anything he has done before. In one way, he is writing about how he sees himself and his uncertainties compared to, say, Sam Beckett. The *nature* of talent, of art, comes winging through. Peter's usual obsession is there: to prove the existence of God and the nature of God. Here He is shown as selfish and uncaring, following His own needs, indifferent to the suffering of man.

20 June For years I have been praying for a sincere radical right-wing play, and this is it, because *Amadeus* is about the uniqueness of talent, its refusal to be part of a system, its refusal to be other than selfish. It celebrates the individual and individuality with a Renaissance fervour.

29 July   Music, like colour, is the most dangerous thing to put in the straight theatre. It generalizes emotion, generates it easily, and ends by dissipating it. And my God, when it's Mozart. . . . You can't easily let *him* into a play.

30 Sept.   It's important we do not present the story entirely through Salieri's eyes. There must be a tension between what the audience sees and what Salieri describes. A difficult balance to achieve. Also, I am more and more interested in the fact that Mozart was not a revolutionary *artist,* but a *social* revolutionary in a feudal world. In many respects he was the first star, the first free-lance − after Handel in London, anyway. Artists at that time were servants, eating below the salt. But Mozart wanted to be a star, wanted to be recognized for his uniqueness, much more than Haydn or Schubert or Beethoven. He was revolutionary in that. He did not want to be just the servant of a nobleman.

12 Oct.   [The principals] all have to play against their natural selves. Paul [Scofield as Salieri] must not be too silky and smooth and general. Simon [Callow] must not sweat as Mozart, there must be no tension in him, he must go for grace and containment. Felicity [Kendal as Constanze] must not be twee, little me-ish, but earthy and comic.

31 Oct.   Paul Scofield said his was the hardest part he had ever tackled in his life. Much harder than Lear because, as Salieri, he was always on stage and had such continuous and alarming changes of tone and concentration.

Peter Hall, *Diaries,* ed John Goodwin (London: Hamish Hamilton, 1983), p. 411, 448, 455, 465, 468, 471

When I read the script I was struck by the operatic quality on two levels − a structural one and an emotional one. Operatic theatre is highly emotional theatre. I told Peter 'I will give you an operatic production'. I tried to emphasize the operatic elements of the play.

Peter Hall, quoted by Harold C. Shonberg, 'Mozart's World: from London to Broadway', *New York Times,* 14 Dec. 1980, Sec. II, p. 1, 35

Simon Callow on playing Mozart

Shaffer had selected − I don't say invented − a brilliantly vivid

Mozart: vulgar, childlike ('infantine,' the text said), hyperactive, ultimately touching, but in many ways unendurable: a show-off, touchy, and ungenerous to fellow-artists. . . . The play isn't a biography of Mozart, and Shaffer was under no obligation to present a full-blown portrait; but what was there, was true. Mozart, if you like, glimpsed by lightning. The role itself, moreover, made a journey from outrage to dejection and finally suffering that was uniquely satisfying. . . .

It was impossible to believe that the little beast I'd produced (in direct response to the text) had written a note of the music around which the whole play revolved. It was equally clear that it would be impossible for an audience to sit and watch this all-farting, all-shrieking monstrosity for more than a few seconds at a time. . . .

Hall had drawn attention to Shaffer's speech patterns in everyday conversation, above all to the cascade of words, and said we should learn from them in our handling of the text: not milking any particular word or phrase, but with a sense of the whole arc of a sentence or a speech. . . .

Quite by chance I picked up Otto Deutsch's hefty *Mozart: a Documentary Biography*. I'd read everything I could get my hands on, but had been daunted by the bulk and dryness of title of this. Within minutes of flicking through its pages, I knew I'd struck gold. There he was, the little bugger, a speaking likeness. Mozart portrayed in letters, memoirs, and laundry bills by his contemporaries. Most of the biographies start from the standpoint of his music; here was the way people really saw him — partisan, sometimes one-sided, but immediately vivid — a picture of a light, tiny, mercurial, volatile, immature, prodigiously energetic, bird-like creature. There were stories of him leaping from the piano-stool to run under the table like a pussy-cat; tapping his fingers incessantly in complex rhythms; making absurd and childish jokes. Much of this is in Peter's play. The beauty of Deutsch's book is that it puts these details in the context of a whole life. . . . The moment I saw this Mozart, Shaffer's text fell into place. Every word, every gesture that he had written was consonant with the man. They simply needed a framework of character to unify them. Once I had found that, the playing style of the piece came easily. Psychological realism was out of the question in view of the kaleidoscopic sequence of scenes. Something akin to revue technique was called for, the capacity to start a scene bang in the middle of it, and to wipe it away as soon as it was finished in order to make room for the quite different emotions of the next. Shaffer's is a theatre of gesture.

The whole body, the mask of the face, ways of speaking, external details are all of the essence of Peter's work. The wig, the giggle, the little hop, and so on. The definitive Shaffer performance was Robert Stephens's Atahuallpa in *The Royal Hunt of the Sun*, pure gesture, voice, movement. It's a linear technique, not in depth — legerdemain the indispensable quality. . . .

The outstanding remaining problem, which I never ceased to work on till the last performance, was to somehow make it credible that the man had written the music. It was essential to believe that inside the giggling, shit-shanking, hyperactive little man was *The Marriage of Figaro*. I listened to the overture to that work morning noon and night. . . .

After six months of playing, a breakthrough occurred: I attained real grace and lightness, instead of striving for it (paradox!), and it became credible that I'd written the music. It was the result of my falling in love. At last I found the courage to be charming. . . .

When I played Mozart, I knew that his tempo and emotional volatility were greatly in excess of mine. As the weeks went by I began to work my own inner speed up to fever pitch. It was deeply exhausting for everyone. I ate my food twice as fast as I'd ever done, I spoke at twice the speed, darted mercurially from place to place, and at the end of the day, all but ran across Waterloo Bridge. If I went for a drink, I drank twice as much as I would normally have done. It was necessary to accustom my body to a completely new metabolic rate.

Simon Callow, *Being an Actor* (Methuen, 1984), p. 84-98, 139

On Salieri

Frank Finlay's Salieri presents a starkly illuminating contrast to Paul Scofield's in the original show. Scofield was a natural aristocrat; robbed of music he would still have been an ornament to the Viennese court. With Mr. Finlay it is all he has got; he is still palpably the small town boy, ungainly and provincial, and hanging on to his job by exclusively professional means. Bargains with God aside, the action shows him fighting for his life.

Irving Wardle, *The Times,* 3 July 1981, p. 11

I knew I could make a new contribution to the part. [Scofield] is twenty years older and concentrates on the old Salieri. I emphasize the younger Salieri. . . . What's difficult is the relation of Salieri with the audience. It is a non-stop operation. Salieri

65

has long monologues and is constantly taking the audience into his confidence. I have to woo the audience. . . . There also are certain demands on the voice. Salieri is a young man at times, an old man at others. That creates some technical problems. The role even has elements of a standup comic.

Ian McKellen, quoted by Harold C. Shonberg, 'Villain of *Amadeus* is Hero of Broadway', *New York Times,* 19 Dec. 1980, Sec. III, p. 3

In Mr. McKellen's superb performance, Salieri's descent into madness was portrayed in dark notes of almost bone-rattling terror. Mr. Wood's protagonist is no less dark, but it's a different kind of darkness: he brings up the nihilistic, absurdist black comedy that is equally implicit in the character's predicament. . . . When Salieri faints while contemplating the unattainable brilliance of Mozart's music, Mr. Wood doesn't so much swoon, as Mr. McKellen did, but instead twirls into a face-first pratfall.

Frank Rich, '*Amadeus,* with Three New Principals', *New York Times,* 17 Dec. 1981, Sec. III, p. 22

The gilt-edged, Rococo world created by Peter Hall, John Bury, and Paul Scofield has the clarity, delicacy, and brilliance of polished glass. The most dazzling feature of this world is an 'ice-blue plastic' stage — a marble-like surface that shifts in colour with changes of light, mirroring with stunning and ghostly effect the sumptuous costumes, the exotic decor, the effete mannerisms, the grace, affectation, beauty, and decadence of the court of Joseph II. Verisimilitude to the court period of the eighteenth century is achieved in part through a magnificent interior proscenium arch, replete with gold leaf, trumpet-blowing cherubs, and filigree. This arch serves as both background and entrance onto a handsome rectangular centre stage, a stage which artfully effects elegance through inlaid wooden panelling set into a marble surface. The symmetrical design of the centre stage backed by the golden proscenium does much to influence and enhance movements that follow classical lines of grace, simplicity, and precision.

James S. Bost, '*Amadeus*', *Theatre Journal,* XXXII (Dec. 1980)

I can admit to being enthralled by his vision of Joseph II's Vienna for almost all of the play's considerable length, because while

Shaffer sometimes passes as a man of ideas he is far more remarkable as a master of the suspension-of-disbelief technique.
[*Amadeus* is] a marvellously engrossing and often amusing
costume thriller, a feast for the eye and the ear, a vehicle for
immense acting performances, and a pretty fair introduction to
the musical genius, if not the personal charms, of W.A. Mozart.
Steve Grant, *The Observer,* 11 Nov. 1979

Shaffer's Mozart is depicted with a dreadful and offensive banality. . . . Mozart is depicted in an offensive and banal way because
he is seen through the eyes of a very, very bad dramatist indeed —
perhaps the worst serious English dramatist since John Drinkwater.
James Fenton, *You Were Marvellous* (London, 1983), p. 30-3

Good ideas don't necessarily result in good plays — especially, as
Equus showed, in Shaffer's hands, Once again Shaffer has had the
acumen to discern a large-scale possibility, and once again he has
reduced it with gimmicks. . . . We all know that Mozart did not
advance, and Shaffer knows we know it, so he had to develop
other elements. He chose two, one factual and one imagined. The
first is the 'revelation' of Mozart's true character, and it's of
limited use. . . . [Salieri] assails the supposed fount of justice,
God. . . . This is Shaffer's second dramatic element, meant to
strengthen Salieri *vis-à-vis* the fascinating Mozart, and in itself it's
an ancient major theme, the calling of divinity to account. But it
crumples Shaffer. At the end of the play's first half, Salieri has a
long speech berating God, which ends: 'To my last breath I shall
block you on earth, as far as I am able.' If the rhetoric is empty,
at least it booms; but then Salieri addresses *us* drily: 'What use,
after all, is Man, if not to teach God his lessons?' The facile
Stoppard-type crack blows away whatever weight Shaffer has
managed to scrape up. Once again the bantam author is giggling
around his Promethean subject.
   The second half of the play is even weaker than the first.
There's no mileage left in the shock of Mozart's character as such,
and Salieri's struggle with God is flimsy, fabricated, facetious. It
all just winds on and down. . . . At the very end the ancient
Salieri totters forward to address us: 'Mediocrities everywhere —
now and to come — I absolve you all! Amen!' Sounds grand, until
one thinks about it. What power of absolution does he have, and
what is he absolving them of? His legacy of jealousy, of a sense of
God's injustice? Of a wish to be more than they are? The best

guess may be that, at the last, Salieri is addressing his author.

Stanley Kauffmann, 'Shaffer's Flat Notes',
Saturday Review, Feb. 1981, p. 78-9

To keep myself entertained during the rather long stretches between selections from Mozart's music, I tried to guess which of his main characters the author identified himself with. Does he see *Amadeus* as a sort of O'Neill and Shaffer, or as a Shaffer and Martinus Scriblerus? Or does he perceive himself as capaciously, magnanimously containing both? There is theatrical know-how in some of this, an undeniable *coup de théâtre* or two, along with such cheap tricks as having the emperor repeatedly say, 'Well, there it is!' — shades of the father in *Equus* with his 'if you perceive my meaning' — and all those cutesy conceits about how this or that famous aria was engendered. . . .

John Simon, 'Amadequus, or Shaffer Rides Again',
New York, 29 Dec. 1980—5 Jan. 1981, p. 62-3

The play's major fault is not intellectual, but structural: it has no second act. Salieri tells us that his quarrel is not with Mozart, but with God. God, however, has not been cast, so we get a succession of scenes from Mozart's last years — scenes which, by the play's own rules, are irrelevant. It doesn't matter how, or even whether, Salieri did for him; his jealousy, once established, is never explored.

Robert Cushman, *The Observer,* 25 Jan. 1981

[The question of the historical accuracy of *Amadeus* has been much debated. Mozart's obscenities (many of them deleted in the revised text) were mostly taken from his letters. Debate continues, however, on whether — whatever the adolescent Mozart *wrote* — he would have spoken in this way. Factual inaccuracy has also been sought, often in a rather petty way. C.J. Gianakaris discusses these issues in 'Fair Play — Peter Shaffer's Treatment of Mozart in *Amadeus*', *Opera News,* 27 Feb. 1982, p. 18, 36. The play was substantially revised for the New York production, and this is now the authorized text.]

One of the faults which I believe existed in the London version was simply that Salieri had too little to do with Mozart's ruin. . . .

In this new American version, he stands where he properly belongs – at the wicked centre of the action. This new, more active Salieri offers himself as a substitute father upon Leopold Mozart's death. He establishes a much closer human contact with Wolfgang. And he finally induces the trusting composer to betray the rituals of the freemasons in *The Magic Flute.* I, of course, took certain obvious liberties with this part of the story. I have no reason whatever to believe that the masons actually repudiated Mozart. . . . The great gain in dramatic terms was that I could now show the (factually true) visit of Salieri and his mistress to a performance of *The Magic Flute.* . . . The main change in *Amadeus,* however, was concerned with the treatment of the Masked Figure who appeared to Mozart to commission a Requiem Mass and whom Mozart in the frenzy of his sick imagination came to regard as the Messenger of Death. In London this figure was actually Salieri's grim manservant Greybig. . . . My unease ended with the total removal of Greybig from the play.

Shaffer, 'Preface' to *Collected Plays,* p. xvii

[The issue of the revision is important because arguably the first version is superior. Both Constanze and Salieri are less complex and developed in the revision.

Two scenes which show Constanze as a protective wife are cut: when she cannot accept that Mozart is working unpaid for Schikaneder when she is unable to 'feed little Karl', and when she tries to tell Mozart the truth about Salieri. Mozart does not listen and says Salieri is a 'really good man'. In the original Mozart sympathetically suggests Constanze leave for Baden (II, xv, 106); in the revision Constanze leaves on her own initiative.

Salieri's part is heavily cut in the revision: his opening monologue is cut by one-third. No longer is information given on such points as (1) Salieri's ideas about the musician as the servant of music rather than a patron (I, iii, 27); (2) the discussion between Salieri, Mozart, and the court about Da Ponte, the librettist (II, iv, 76-7); (3) Salieri's continuous efforts to prevent the production of *Marriage of Figaro* (II, iv, 80); (4) Salieri's knowledge that Mozart 'was now disposed to believe me his friend. I could now attack him unsuspected. Could my Enemy possibly *intend* this?' (II, vi, 85); (5) the conversation in which Salieri tells Mozart that he knows of his back-stabbing gossip (II, viii, 91-2); (6) Salieri's realization that his anger with Mozart is such that he has 'to end it' (II, x, 97); (7) Salieri's account of his offering to help Count Walsegg commission the Requiem from Mozart (II, xv, 104-5); (8) Salieri's important line, 'If I cannot be Mozart, I do not wish to be anything' (II, xx, 120). The revisions are dealt with in detail by C.J. Gianakaris, 'Shaffer's Revisions in *Amadeus', Theatre Journal,* XXV (1983), p. 88-101.]

On the film

[Milos Forman and I] spent well over four months together in a Connecticut farmhouse — five days a week, twelve hours a day — seeing virtually no other company. These were four months of sustained work, punctuated by innumerable tussles, flatterings, and depressions, but also by sudden gleeful breakthroughs to relieve the monotony of the prevalent uncertainty. . . . We acted out countless versions of each scene, improvising them aloud. . . . We are also blatantly claiming the grand licence of the storyteller to embellish his tale with fictional ornament, and — above all — to supply it with a climax whose sole justification need be that it enthralls his audience and emblazons his theme. . . .

To me there is something pure about Salieri's pursuit of an eternal Absolute through music, just as there is something irredeemably impure about his simultaneous pursuit of eternal fame. The yoking of these two clearly opposed drives led us finally to devise a climax totally different from that of the play: a nightlong encounter between the physically dying Mozart and the spiritually ravenous Salieri, motivated entirely by the latter's crazed lust to snatch a piece of divinity for himself. Quite obviously, such a scene never took place in fact. However, our concern at this point was not with fact, but with the undeniable laws of drama. . . .

The motif of masked people goes all through the picture — paralleling to some extent Mozart's own preoccupation with them. After all, the three great Da Ponte operas (*The Marriage of Figaro, Don Giovanni,* and *Cosi fan tutte*) are all concerned with the dramatic effects of wearing disguise. What pleased me best about this resolution is that we were able to construct a scene that is highly effective in cinematic terms, yet wholly concerned with the least visual of all possible subjects: *music itself.* . . .

Filming *Amadeus* for six months in Czechoslovakia was a testing but perhaps indispensable experience, considering our subject. Prague offers the most complete baroque and rococo setting in Europe.

Shaffer, 'Introduction to the Film Edition' (Signet/
New American Library, 1984) p. xiii-xxi

The movie's Salieri is at once more single-mindedly obsessive and less unpleasant than the stage one. And, aged, long-forgotten, *in extremis,* he tells his story to his youthful confessor in Vienna's madhouse. So from the start we're close up to, invited into the deranged mind of, the protagonist-narrator. The pair of gossip-mongering *venticelli,* who acted as stage chorus, have been dropped. So too has Salieri's wife, to give the impression of his being celibate. Two substantial characters have been added – Mozart's father, Leopold, and the actor-manager of the popular music-hall that commissioned *The Magic Flute,* Emanuel Schikaneder. . . . In paring the text, Shaffer has cut all the references to masonry, toned down Mozart's infantile scatology, and trimmed the cultural name-dropping and musicological asides. . . . In their determination to make *Amadeus* a cinematic experience, Shaffer and Forman have produced a psychologically stronger dramatic line than the play had. The wounds Mozart inflicts on Salieri – as even the most cloth-eared members of the movie audience will recognize – are musical ones; the final phase of Salieri's campaign of destruction utilizes the brilliant insights he has into the functions of guilt and of disguise in Mozart's operas. . . . There are many visual felicities – not least an unforgettable cut from the five-year-old prodigy Mozart performing blindfold before some royal audience to the teenage Salieri playing a carefree game of blind-man's buff with the other kids in the streets of Legnano.

Philip French, *The Observer,* 20 Jan. 1985

What I miss most is the towering, maniacal obsessiveness of Salieri's relationship with Mozart. In the theatre, Salieri talked Iago-like to us: in the cinema he is a knobbly old party sitting in what looks like a Viennese madhouse confessing his story to the hospital chaplain. The difference is crucial. In the theatre, even if we couldn't go along with Salieri's desire to avenge himself on God by striking at Mozart, we were implicated in his jealousy and shared his mediocrity. In the cinema we simply become interested spectators of a curious love-hate relationship. . . . Shaffer and Forman seem to have Salieri a more kempt and cool figure than in the original. . . . Shaffer's play was about a man trying to kill God: Forman's film is more about the tribulations of a musical revolutionary. . . . The shift towards Mozart makes the film a more conventional study of a harassed innovator: the play was a much stranger piece about cancerous envy and gnawing mediocrity.

Michael Billington, *The Guardian,* 17 Jan. 1985

A selection of other articles and reviews

Robert Asahina, 'Theatre Chronicle', *Hudson Review,* XXXIV (Summer 1981), p. 263-8.

Roland Gelatt, 'Peter Shaffer's *Amadeus:* a Controversial Hit', *Saturday Review,* Nov. 1980, p. 11-14.

C.J. Gianakaris, 'Drama into Film: the Shaffer Situation', *Modern Drama,* XXVIII (March 1985), p. 83-98.

C.J. Gianakaris, 'A Playwright Looks at Mozart: Peter Shaffer's *Amadeus', Comparative Drama,* XV (Spring 1981), p. 37-53.

Werner Huber and Hubert Zapf, 'On the Structure of Peter Shaffer's *Amadeus', Modern Drama,* XXVII (1984), p. 299-313.

Michiko Katutani, 'How *Amadeus* was Translated from Play to Film', *New York Times,* 16 Sept. 1984, Sec. II, p. 1, 20.

Dennis A. Klein, *'Amadeus:* the Third Part of Peter Shaffer's Dramatic Trilogy', *Modern Language Studies,* XIII (1983), p. 31-8.

Paul Henry Lang, 'Salvaging Salieri (and Mozart) after *Amadeus', Opus,* Oct. 1985, p. 18-21.

Janet Karsten Larson, *'Amadeus:* Shaffer's Hollow Men', *Christian Century,* XCVIII (May 1981), p. 578-83.

Glenn M. Loney, 'Re-creating *Amadeus:* an American Team Re-creates John Bury's Designs', *Theatre Crafts,* March 1981, p. 10-13, 65-8, 70, 72, 74-5.

J.D. McClatchy, 'A Little More Night Music', *Yale Review,* LXXIII (Oct. 1983), p. 115-22.

Frank X. Mikels and James Rurak, 'Finishing Salieri', *Soundings,* LVII (Spring 1984), p. 42-54.

Matthew Scott, *'Amadeus:* a Glimpse of the Absolute Theatre', *Plays and Players,* Feb. 1980, p. 40-1.

Samuel Terrien, *'Amadeus* Revisited', *Theology Today,* XLII (1986), p. 435-43.

Carol Wootton, 'Literary Portraits of Mozart', *Mosaic* (Winnipeg), XVII (Fall 1985), p. 77-84.

Yonadab

Play in two acts.

First London production: Olivier Th., 4 Dec. 1985 (dir. Peter Hall; with Alan Bates as Yonadab, Patrick Stewart as David, and Wendy Morgan as Tamar).

Unpublished.

Yonadab, narrator and main character, persuades his cousin Amnon of the rightness of his incestuous love for Tamar, justifying rape by quoting the customs of neighbouring Egypt, where royal siblings mate and become divine in the process. The result is disappointment, needless to say, which turns infatuation into hate. Amnon throws out Tamar who wanders the streets of Jerusalem stark naked . . . advertising her shame, and finding her way, as if by accident, to the house of Absalom. This is not part of Yonadab's scheme and he begins to suspect that a greater author than himself is taking over the plot. . . . Threatened by Absalom, Yonadab drops similar poison in his ear. He invents certain prophecies that lead the credulous to the conclusion that both Absalom and Tamar are ordained. Absalom makes that jump and Yonadab – to his surprise – follows him. For Tamar seems to offer independent confirmation of the dreams he has described. What he doesn't know . . . is that Tamar has become as adept behind the arras as himself, listening as he tempts Absalom. Like Aaron, he believes that our greatest desire is to see gods walking upon the earth, and like that tainted priest he denies the second commandment. He wants to lose himself, to be dazzled and dissolved in visible splendour. Instead he is bathed in the blood of his relatives as Tamar – her consciousness raised and her conscience erased by her defilement – completes her terrible revenge. Yonadab, faced with Amnon, the naked idealist, dead and covered with the dung of a donkey, and Absalom hanging by his hair between heaven and earth, not surprisingly remembers his humanity and renounces all creeds.

Clive Sinclair, *Times Literary Supplement,*
20 Dec. 1985, p. 1457

This play owes its existence primarily to two sources: the Book of Samuel which I first read as a boy, and the book of Dan Jacobson called *The Rape of Tamar* which I first encountered in 1970. To read this modern novel, so elegantly and yet so seriously concerned with an ancient text, is to watch the ray of a scrutinizing intelligence play over the implacable slab of a grim old monument. The experience started in me a strong desire to make a drama out of these same materials. The terrible directness of the original Testament attracted me as deeply as the emotional paradox discernible under the surface of the novel: the longing for creed in the incredulous, the profound ache for belief in the mockers of belief. I made many notes on how possibly the play could be formed; but other work intervened and time passed. Always however through fifteen years the desire remained with me.

Last year I unearthed my notes and re-read them. To my excited nose they exuded the unmistakable scent of demand: *write this now*! On impulse I contacted Mr. Jacobson, whom I had once met briefly, and to whom I had confided my hopes. We renewed our acquaintance for a similarly brief hour: sufficient time however to learn how pleased he was by the renewal of my enthusiasm, and to explore our joint recognition that a play inspired by, but not totally based on, a novel must finally differ radically from it in many places.

This of course became increasingly evident as I began work in earnest. All the impulses which had led me to choose the story took over, transforming it. As the play evolved, so did my need to create more material entirely different: to endow it in fact with independent life. It was an extraordinary experience, to feel the piece feeding gratefully on its main source and then gradually taking off on its own: moving as instinct dictated, and finally flying away into new intention and completely new story. Once again I experienced the discomforting and exhilarating realization that the reasons one writes a play are not all immediately apparent when one begins it.

Throughout, I have cherished the pleasure which started me off: the ray of light playing on the slab. Perhaps that is why, finally, the dominant image in my head has not been a blood-thirsty but an ambiguous one of curtains: a girl, carried through a labyrinth of stone streets hidden behind the curtains of her litter; the endless curtains of the Middle East, hiding what must not be looked on: secret beds and sacred cupboards. And above all, the many different kinds of curtain suspended before the eyes of my protagonist − Yonadab the Watcher.

Shaffer, programme note to the National Theatre production

If I had plunged into biblical scholarship I might well never have re-emerged. Besides, not a great deal is known about the period. For Mozart you have Jahn, you have Deutsch, and a hundred others. But where do you find the insights into Davidic society? There will be the usual charges of historical inaccuracies. But it is the jump into the unknown, that is the challenge, the pleasure, and the fun. . . . I see Yonadab as the bridge between the Old

Testament and our own society. He does the explaining and the narrating. . . .

  Yonadab is not grand in the sense that *Royal Hunt* was. The early play had to be: it was, after all, about a society made of gold. The society of King David was more famed for power than splendour. But I still believe in spectacle and I certainly want the eye to have a good evening as well as the ear. Let's say that it is an austere eyeful.

Shaffer, quoted by John Higgins, *The Times,* 28 Nov. 1985

Yonadab draws examples from ancient Egypt where the pharaohs, in their union between brother and sister, became demigods. It was the passion that was the privilege of those chosen to rule. It was also practised among the Egyptians to keep the blood pure, to give you a special wisdom. With purity of blood comes purity of mind. So Amnon becomes convinced that he will attain divinity.

Shaffer, quoted by Clare Colvin, *Drama,* 1986 (1), p. 11

A long, louche literary entertainment which relates to serious drama rather as Little Red Riding Hood relates to anthropology. You can, if you're so inclined, read into it a parable on vicarious experience, or the terrors of heterosexual lust; but really, it's only about a man who gets a grim kick out of watching his cousin having it off with his sister. Like all Shaffer's plays, *Yonadab* is theatrical without being dramatic. By this I mean that it is inspired by a sensational situation which is then unfolded layer by layer like Ibsen's onion, and, like the same vegetable, is found to have no real centre. What is missing is the sense of progress and discovery, which is the essence of drama. The fact that there is a story with a beginning and an end is secondary to the purely theatrical thrill of watching the situation. The situation is the message: theatre as voyeurism. . . . Shaffer ends up with a slack and purient literary melodrama of sexual revenge.

John Peter, *Sunday Times,* 8 Dec. 1985, p. 43

We come away possibly no nearer to knowing why God's word should lead men to such cruelties, or why man's cruelty should lead us amazingly to God's words. Yet the questions gnaw relentlessly into our conscience and that, surely, is the mark of a fine and fulfilling play.

Jack Tinker, *Daily Mail,* 5 Dec. 1985

The real objection to the play is that it lays claim to ultimate questions of man's place in the universe and reduces them simply to a theatrical structure.

Irving Wardle, *The Times*, 5 Dec. 1985

The audience is thus invited to suspend its disbelief (not an easy matter, given Yonadab's anachronisms) and accept that it is at the court of King David. The trouble is, both writer and director seem to lack the necessary conviction. David comes over as a cross between Atahuallpa and King Lear, beautiful Absalom looks as if he belongs at a Band Aid jamboree and Amnon behaves like Captain Hook.

Clive Sinclair, as above

Shaffer has, however, always been a powerful image-maker and Peter Hall's production makes the most of the play's visual possibilities. John Bury has designed a set of translucent curtains imprinted with the Hebraic alphabet that plausibly translates us into David's Jerusalem. And, without lapsing into Cecil B. De Millery, Hall creates an atmosphere of despotism and sensuality: the rape is evoked through projected shadows and the climactic slaughter at Baal-hazor has the right feel of a wild ritual turning to blood-drenched chaos. . . .

I was also reminded of Yeats's remark about rhetoric being the will striving to do the work of the imagination. Time and again one hears Shaffer (a natural storyteller) trying to inflate the theme through heightened language. After the crucial rape, Amnon utters a piercing cry indicating that he 'topples down the long incline of himself'. I simply don't know what that means. Amnon is also victim, we are told, of 'the archaic alphabet of lust'. But how can the monomaniac drive of the rapist have alphabetic diversity? And when Bates's Yonadab suggests we all want to see 'gods walking on earth', my reaction is to ask if that is true.

Michael Billington, *The Guardian*, 6 Dec. 1985

Yonadab occurs some 2,500 years before *The Royal Hunt of the Sun*, 2,700 before *Amadeus* and 2,900-odd before *Equus*, yet brings together ideas and obsessions to be found in all three.

There's the envious outsider, the man who feels himself emotionally and spiritually deprived, yearning to acquire the capacities, gifts, and strengths he believes another unjustly to have been given. There's the reaching for an ecstasy which invariably turns out to be impure, imperfect, flawed, or failed in some way. There's the outrage at a universe that's perverse or empty or perversely empty: a paradoxical mix of atheism and wishfulness rather similar to that expressed by Beckett's Hamm, for whom God was 'that bastard — he doesn't even exist'. There's the hope, invariably disappointed, that somehow human beings will so harness the twin powers of love and creativity as themselves to become gods on earth. . . .

Shaffer isn't content to let his action take its own course and suggest its own meaning. He doesn't trust it adequately to cope with his obsessions, still less draw conclusions from them. At any rate, he's all too evidently omnipresent himself, commenting and arguing and interpreting and adjudicating in a style that's sometimes nudging and colloquial, sometimes sententious and sermonizing, but either way leaves us in the audience scant space to indulge what little capacity for intellectual speculation we ourselves might possess.

What's worse, his chosen mouthpiece or megaphone is a single character, one who dominates the evening without being very plausible or interesting in himself: Yonadab. The psychiatrist Dysart in *Equus* and the composer Salieri in *Amadeus* were both expected to narrate their respective stories and bring out those stories' significance; but each of them could also claim some consistency of character, and the latter a certain sombre fascination as well. That's not the case with Yonadab, who seems a Biblical Iago or Mephistopheles, an anachronistic version of the archetypal man-in-the-dirty-mac, a humanist idealist and searcher-after-truth, and a sardonically alienated rebel, depending on how Shaffer is feeling and what his plot is wanting.

Benedict Nightingale, *New Statesman,* 13 Dec. 1985, p. 31-2

It is about the conflict between cold calculation and dangerous ecstasy with God as the invisible protagonist. But this time you can hear Shaffer audibly cranking up the material to fit his governing obsession. . . . I emerged, however, reflecting that *Yonadab* is Shaffer's fifth play on the same basic theme. He is a fine dramatist but I wish he would temporarily banish God from his theatrical vocabulary and translate his direct experience of life into drama rather than seek out stories that tally with his own fixations.

Michael Billington, as above

The Salt Land

Play for television.
First transmitted: ITV, 8 Nov. 1955.
Unpublished.

The scenes are set on a ship taking illegal immigrants to Palestine in 1947, at a command post at war with Arabs in 1948, and on a struggling settlement in the Negev in Israel in 1949. Two brothers are bitterly in conflict about the best future for Israel: finally Arieh murders his younger brother, Jo.

The Salt Land is about two brothers, each with a dream for the State of Israel, each with an ulterior motive: Arieh, who wants to recreate the Garden of Eden in the middle of the Negev desert, but whose motivations are pride and stubbornness; and Jo, who wants to see the people of Israel living with dignity, but who is motivated by ambition and greed. It is the story of a father who suffers disillusionment over his sons: one because he has turned to crime in order to realize his dream, and the other because he comes to put material goals before Jewish law. And it is about a young wife watching her husband — and her marriage — falling apart.

Dennis A. Klein, *Peter Shaffer,* p. 24

[In] *The Salt Land* I attempted to construct a tragedy along loosely classical lines, not for the sake of experiment, though experiment has its own fascination, but because the subject of Israel and immigration is truly heroic, and deserves classical treatment.

Shaffer, 'Labels Aren't for Playwrights,' p. 21

A patchily-worked out though serious and well constructed attempt to present a classical tragedy situation in terms of modern Israel.

John Russell Taylor, *Anger and After*
(revised ed., Methuen, 1969), p. 273

The Prodigal Father

Play for radio.
First transmitted: BBC, 14 Sept. 1957.
Unpublished.

Leander Johnson is considering buying a stately home for his son, Jed, from Lady Sylvia Glenister, who is forced to sell it. Jed, brought up by his mother and unhappy through his childhood, has not seen his father for sixteen years. Lady Sylvia keeps Lucy, a young orphan, in the house. Leander ultimately decides not to buy the house, but hopes to see Lady Sylvia again. Father and son are reconciled, at least temporarily, and Lucy will write to Jed.

Balance of Terror

Play for television.
First transmitted: BBC, 21 Nov. 1957.
Unpublished: script lost.

Balance of Terror *is on the level of a second feature film; its action, sweetened by a romantic interlude, consists of the double-cross, the bluff, and the double-bluff. . . . . The hero of* Balance of Terror, *a British spy who discovers almost too late that his Whitehall chief is a Russian agent, is at the centre of a situation Mr. Shaffer has tangled with careful stealth and which he unravels with energetic dexterity. But although the plot is soundly built its effectiveness is much diminished by the failure of characters to respond naturally to situations: events, therefore, generate no atmosphere.*

The Times, 22 Nov. 1957, p. 8

Detective novels

The Woman in the Wardrobe (as Peter Antony). Evans, 1951. [Many bibliographies give this novel as a collaboration.]

How Doth the Little Crocodile? (as Peter Antony, with Anthony Shaffer). Evans, 1952; New York: Macmillan, 1957.

Withered Murder (with Anthony Shaffer). Gollancz, 1955; New York: Macmillan, 1956.

In England there is now a definite attempt to create a two-party system, and playwrights tend to be assigned automatically to the Right or Left by journalists, and even by some critics, anxious to establish a pattern of some sort that, by its mere existence, will make them feel more secure. . . . Uncertainty within myself is something I prize. I do not want to classify, or be classified by others, especially since the classifications are not only irrelevant but often quite perverse. A superb rhetorician like John Osborne is identified as a social realist; the essential blindness of the true virtuoso executant is hailed as social awareness; a baroque concerto like *Look Back in Anger,* for solo voice and conventional tutti, is praised as twelve-tone music. . . .

As a playwright, I'm scared of the too well-defined identity − of being either publicly or (even worse) privately its prisoner. I rather believe my totem animal to be the chameleon. At any rate, if I knew how to formulate it, I would like to propound an Artistic Theory of Indeterminacy. . . . I am beginning to be uneasy about a climate of belief that makes me feel a slight guilt because I want to do many different kinds of things

in the theatre. Just as I worked deliberately in the deadened convention of week-end-cottage naturalism in *Five Finger Exercise*
(but without any desire to be tricksy; the convention is utterly
appropriate to the subject, and far from dead if handled with
seriousness and desire), so I want to work in other conventions
and forms that attract me. . . . I'm radical enough, too, to believe
that almost all the new English plays produced in the West End
of London since I was born have been decadent or worthless.

'Labels Aren't for Playwrights', Feb. 1960, p. 20-1

Between actors and playwrights exists, at best, a violent, desperate,
irrefragable relation which makes reconciliation in a conventional
sense impossible between them, and even undesirable. It is perhaps the most profoundly loving, because the most urgently
needful, of all relations — that between hungry beings and their
prey. Over the years my simple view of actors, as a jolly company
of people to be wistfully envied, changed and deepened as I came
to see their exclusiveness and their ultimate indifference to
writers as something infinitely more profound than mere trade
unionism. . . .

The rehearsal of a serious play is an elaborate and quietly
awful ceremony of fertilization; a ritual, despite its frequent
appearance of disorganization and its very real air of friendliness,
of sacrifice and rebirth. At the beginning, the playwright is
accepted as God-King; he is felt to contain some truth without
which the players cannot live. . . . Gradually the actors gain
strength — his strength: they learn his words, his secrets; they
cut off his hair. They take away everything he has, at first tenta-
tively, and then boldly, with increasing assurance. . . . They need
his potency, and do not rest — cannot rest — until they have it.
*For the actor dies between roles, and comes to work seeking his
spring.* . . .

Actors will tell you, and tell you rightly, that they can do
nothing until they have thrown away the text — until, that is,
they have thrown away you, until there does not survive a single
punctuation mark to remind them of your vanished power, or a
word remaining undissolved in their blood streams. And when
this happens, you feel your death. You are the least needed
person in the theatre; you are totally superfluous. . . .

What is [the actor's] article of faith? It is simple and immense.
Every man contains in himself the history of man. . . . . [The
actor] has therefore an almost divine function in society, for to
survive as a true speaker for us he must find in himself what most

of us deny is there — the experience of the race. . . . The moral purpose of actors, which is the exorcism not only of playwrights but of society, can be accomplished only by slaying the mortal enemy of truth, preconception. And in the same degree the playwright does likewise. This is where we meet, on moral ground.

'The Cannibal Theatre', Oct. 1960

All art is autobiographical inasmuch as it refers to personal experience. . . . The torment of adolescence is in all the plays, as is the essential pessimism in the face of certain death. These tensions and obsessions are autobiographical. But of course they are dressed up as stories, myths. That is theatre. . . . I do lots and lots of drafts until they become lighter, less concerned, in the Inca play, with reality, more with essentials. The last version is the most meaningful. . . .

As the man said, there are many tunes yet to be written in C major. And there are many plays yet to be written in a living room. As far as the form being old-fashioned, I suppose it is. But *Look Back in Anger* is just as old-fashioned in form. Anyway, form is dictated by content. . . . Keeping up with fashion is a terrible race. Fashion consciousness is superficial. I'm very grateful for the training I've had with these two plays [*Five Finger Exercise* and the double-bill]. I've learned how to tell a story, draw characters, devise plausible entrances and exits. I've acquired a technique to stand me in good stead for the greater and less charted seas of semi- and expressionistic theatre.

Interview in *Behind the Scenes*, from 1963

If one wishes to reproduce exactly the timbre of a human experience on the stage, this is very difficult because, as we all know, nothing is the same twice. Our lives are completely unrepeatable. Moments are unrepeatable, sex is unrepeatable, everything. The stage, by implying a kind of formulation, implies repeatability. The author's problem is to find words that will have much of the same vitalizing effect every time they're spoken. Great poetry does this, second-rate poetry never does it. . . .

When [Artaud] says the psychological drama is dead, this seems to me to be absolutely rubbish — it has hardly begun. . . . The danger in modern theatre is that it has elaborated the most stunning techniques — certainly verbally. Pinter is the obvious example of this extraordinary musicianship in writing and the conjuring up of atmospheres, but with each advance the disappointing thing is the scale becomes more and more miniature, more and more private, there's a kind of retreat into fetish and the private sex-games with your wife. . . . Obviously no one was embarrassed by, say, 'To be or not to be'. Everything involved in the idea of that speech has been lost in the English theatre at the moment and one of the reasons for this is a curious English sense that it's not very good taste to talk about religion and politics. . . . Good taste consists of not examining universal questions.

'Artaud for Artaud's Sake', May-June 1964

Most comedies aren't funny enough. I believe they should be *hysterically* funny. The trouble is that farce has been destroyed by the permissive society. The best of them — by Feydeau, for example — are about people whose conventional standards are being assaulted by some awful embarrassment. But now there's no embarrassment. Anything goes.

[Storytelling is] an essential part of the playwright's business. I think one should love the audience, but not pander to it. If you don't engage them they stay in their houses or their bed-sitters, watching television, rather than come to the theatre and be told a story. And they need to be there. It's a need as basic as sex. . . . I passionately believe that people come to the theatre to be surprised, moved, illuminated. They're not interested simply in what they're *hearing*. They're receiving what you say viscerally. I remember watching a storyteller in the market at Marakesh. The audience probably knew the story as well as he did. But they were rapt, absorbed. He sensed their hunger and he was satisfying it.

'Shaffer Gallops to Glory and Explains What Makes Him Run',
29 July 1973

One is not finally aware of why one idea insisted and the others dropped away. The playwright hopes that one will say 'Write me, write me'. That's what happened with *Equus*. . . .

The difference between that boy [in *Equus*] leaping up and down out of darkness like a fish out of water, striking at those heads [of the horses], naked or in a sweater and jeans, seems to me like the difference between poetry and prose on stage. One is an unforgettable image and the other is, well, small and uninteresting in comparison.

'Why Are there Two Us in *Equus*?', 13 Apr. 1975, p. 26, 28

Oriental theatre excited me. Japanese Noh actors contemplate their masks before putting them on, investing them with a psychic energy. I wanted to capture that. I have been accused of being theatrical, but maybe those critics are not aware of how many hours of labour it takes to be theatrical. That is what I want to be; after all, I work in the theatre. It is not a derogatory term.

'Psychic Energy', Feb. 1980, p. 13

England is the best place for a playwright to be because there has always been a passionate devotion to drama and to the profundity of acting in the English character. There is always some slight element of self-consciousness about other countries. We, a so-called self-conscious people, have had no difficulty ever in what you would have thought would be the most self-conscious activity in the world, acting. It may be a form of hiding, I don't know.

Actors are the walking encyclopaedias of human experience. They dig into themselves to find their psyche. We have it from the village hall right up to the National Theatre. In England we have always wanted to have a go at acting, cherished the art of acting and indeed the art of writing for the theatre. . . .

There is in me a continuous tension between what I suppose I could call the Apollonian and the Dionysiac sides of interpreting life, between, say, Dysart and Alan Strang. It immediately begins to sound high falutin', when one talks about it oneself — I don't really see it in those dry intellectual terms. I just feel in myself that there is a constant debate going on between the violence of instinct on the one hand and the desire in my mind for order and restraint. . . .

I love that word playwright, particularly *wright* — it suggests a wheelwright or cartwright, a man with a hammer, hammering out a solid structure, and I've always tried to do that. I like to bury all my labour and effort so that it appears to be effortless.

'The Two Sides of Theatre's Agonised Perfectionist', 28 Apr. 1980

[*Royal Hunt, Equus,* and *Amadeus*] possess certain features in common. Each owns a certain flamboyance: a reliance upon gesture to enshrine idea — without which there is no theatre; a desire to enthrall a crowd of watchers — without which there is certainly no theatre; and a strong pleasure in illusion. I imagine that this pleasure has always been a motive with me, ever since as a young boy I laid out a pack of cards on my pillow in bed, and imagined the lives of the Kings, Queens and Jacks rather than play games with them. It is my object to tell tales; to conjure the spectres of horror and happiness, and fill other heads with the images which have haunted my own. My desire, I suppose, is to perturb and make gasp: to please and make laugh: to surprise. If I am a peacock in this respect, at least I am aware that peacockery is one of the dramatist's obligations.

'A Personal Essay', *The Royal Hunt of the Sun,*
ed. Peter Cairns (Longman, 1983), p. vi-vii

a: Primary Sources

The Collected Plays, with a Preface (New York: Harmony, 1982). [Publication details of individual plays may be found under their titles in Section 2.]

Articles and Essays

'Labels Aren't for Playwrights', *Theatre Arts,* XLIV (Feb. 1960), p. 20-1.

'The Cannibal Theatre', *Atlantic Monthly,* CCVI (Oct. 1960), p. 48-50.

'Artaud for Artaud's Sake', *Encore,* No. 49 (May-June 1964), p. 20-31. [Participant in discussion on 'theatre of cruelty'.]

'In Search of a God', *Plays and Players,* Oct. 1964, p. 22. [On *Royal Hunt.*]

'Peter Shaffer's Personal "Dialogue",' *New York Times,* 24 Oct. 1965, Sec. II, p. 1, 3. [In form of self-interview.]

'To See the Soul of a Man', *New York Times,* 24 Oct. 1965, Sec. II, p. 3.

'End of Empire', *The Listener,* 13 Aug. 1970, p. 220-1. [Review of *The Conquest of the Incas,* by John Hemming: relevant for *Royal Hunt.*]

'What We Owe to Britten', *Sunday Times,* 18 Nov. 1973, p. 35 [Sixtieth birthday tribute to the composer.]

'*Equus*: Playwright Peter Shaffer Interprets its Ritual', *Vogue,* CLXV (Feb. 1975), p. 136, 192.

'Figure of Death', *The Observer,* 4 Nov. 1979, p. 37. [Images shaping *Amadeus* and other plays.]

'Scripts in Trans-Atlantic Crossings May Suffer Two Kinds of Changes', *Dramatists Guild Quarterly,* Spring 1980, p. 29-33.

'Salieri Was Really the Only Choice', *New York Times,* 14 Oct. 1984, Sec. II, p. 8. [Letter.]

'Mozartian Magic behind the Masks', *The Times,* 16 Jan. 1985, p. 9. [*Amadeus,* stage and film.]

Interviews

W.L. Webb, 'Committed to Nothing but the Theatre,' *Manchester Guardian,* 27 Aug. 1959. p. 4.

Joseph A. Loftus, 'Playwright's Moral Exercise', *New York Times,* 29 Nov. 1959, Sec. II, p. 1, 3.

John Russell Taylor, 'Shaffer and the Incas', *Plays and Players,* Apr. 1964, p. 12-3.

Barbara Gelb, 'And Its Author', *New York Times,* 14 Nov. 1965, Sec. II, p. 1, 2, 4.

Barry Pree, 'Peter Shaffer', in *Behind the Scenes,* ed. Joseph McCrindle (Pitman, 1971), p. 205-10 (reprinted from *Transatlantic Review,* Autumn 1963).

Philip Oakes, 'Shaffer Gallops to Glory and Explains what Makes Him Run', *Sunday Times,* 29 July 1973, p. 33.

Christopher Ford, 'High Horse', *The Guardian,* 6 Aug. 1973, p. 8.

Mel Gussow, 'Shaffer Details a Mind's Journey in *Equus*', *New York Times,* 24 Oct. 1974, p. 50.

Tom Buckley, 'Why Are There Two Us in "Equus"?', *New York Times,* Magazine, 13 Apr. 1975, p. 20-1, 25-6, 28, 30, 32, 34, 37-8, 40.

Peter Adam, 'Peter Shaffer on Faith, Farce, and Masks', *The Listener,* 14 Oct. 1976, p. 476-7.

Colin Chambers, 'Psychic Energy', *Plays and Players,* Feb. 1980, p. 11-13.

Brian Connell, 'The Two Sides of Theatre's Agonized Perfectionist', *The Times,* 28 Apr. 1980, p. 7.

Harold C. Schoenberg, 'Mozart's World: From London to Broadway', *New York Times,* 14 Dec. 1980, Sec. II, p. 1, 35.

David Gillard, 'Deadly Rivals', *Radio Times,* 22-28 Jan. 1983, p. 4. [Brief, on *Amadeus.*]

Roland Gelatt, 'Mostly *Amadeus*', *Horizon,* Sept. 1984, p. 49-52.

John Higgins, 'The Challenge of Jumping into the Unknown', *The Times,* 28 Nov. 1985, p. 15. [*Yonadab.*]

Clare Colvin, 'Quest for Perfection', *Drama,* 1986 (1), p. 11-12.

b: Secondary Sources

Full-length Studies

John Russell Taylor, *Peter Shaffer.* Longman, for the British Council, 1974 ('Writers and Their Work' series).

Dennis A. Klein, *Peter Shaffer.* Boston, Mass.: G.K. Hall, 1979 (Twayne English Authors).

Articles and Chapters in Books

Ralph S. Carlson, 'Peter Shaffer', *Critical Survey of Drama,* IV, ed. Frank N. Magill (Englewood Cliffs, N.J.: Salem Press, 1985), p. 1676-88.

John M. Clum, 'Religion and Five Contemporary Plays: the Quest for God in a Godless World', *South Atlantic Quarterly,* LXXVII (1978), p. 418-32. [Parts on *Royal Hunt* and *Equus.*]

Joan F. Dean, 'The Family as Microcosm in Shaffer's Plays', *Ball State University Forum,* XXIII, No. 1 (1982), p. 30-4.

Joan F. Dean, 'Peter Shaffer's Recurrent Character Type', *Modern Drama,* XXI (Sept. 1978), p. 297-306.

John Elsom, 'Peter Shaffer', *Contemporary Dramatists,* ed. James Vinson (London: Macmillan, 3rd ed., 1982), p. 708-11.

C.J. Gianakaris, 'Theatre of the Mind in Miller, Osborne, and Shaffer', *Renascence,* XXX (1977), p. 33-42.

Michael Gillespie, 'Peter Shaffer: "To Make whatever God There Is",' *Claudel Studies,* III, No. 2 (1982), p. 61-70.

Ronald Hayman, *British Theatre since 1955: a Reassessment* (Oxford, 1979), p. 52-5.

Michael Hindin, 'When Playwrights Talk to God: Peter Shaffer and the Legacy of O'Neill', *Comparative Drama,* XVI (Spring 1982), p. 49-63.

Oleg Kerensky, *The New British Drama,* (London: Hamish Hamilton, 1977), p. 31-58.

Dennis A. Klein, 'Literary Onomastics in Peter Shaffer's *Shrivings* and *Equus', Literary Onomastics Studies,* VII (1980), p. 127-38.

Barbara Lounsberry, ' "God-hunting": the Chaos of Worship in Peter Shaffer's *Equus* and *Royal Hunt of the Sun', Modern Drama,* XXI (1978), p. 13-28.

Charles A. Pennel, 'The Plays of Peter Shaffer: Experiments in Convention', *Kansas Quarterly,* III, No. 2 (1971), p. 100-09.

Rodney Simard, *Postmodern Drama: Contemporary Playwrights in America and Britain* (University Press of America, 1984). [Seeks a postmodern dramatic aesthetic in Shaffer and others.]

Warren Sylvester Smith, 'Peter Shaffer', *British Dramatists since World War Two,* ed. Stanley Weintraub, *Dictionary of Literary Biography, Vol. 13* (Detroit, Mich.: Gale, 1982), p. 451-69.

James R. Stacy, 'The Sun and the Horse: Peter Shaffer's Search for Worship', *Educational Theatre Journal,* XXVIII (1976), p. 325-37.

Tom Sutcliffe, 'The Secret of Shaffer's Success', *The Guardian,* 9 July 1982, p. 9.

John Russell Taylor, 'Art and Commerce', in *Contemporary English Drama,* ed. C.W.E. Bigsby (London: Edward Arnold, 1981), p. 178-81 (Stratford-upon-Avon Studies, No. 19).

Reference Sources

Kimball King, *Twenty Modern British Playwrights: a Bibliography, 1956 to 1976.* New York: Garland, 1977, p. 197-206.

Dennis A. Klein, *Peter and Anthony Shaffer: a Reference Guide.* Boston, Mass.: G.K. Hall, 1982.

DATE DUE
